Coloring Book
Flowers

This book belong to :

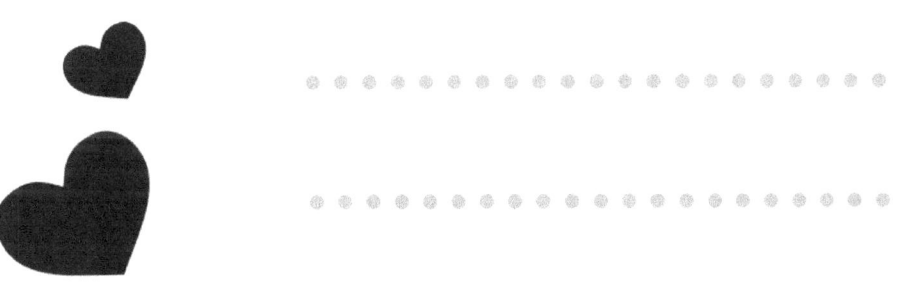

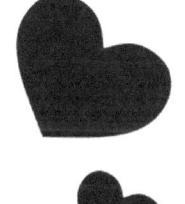

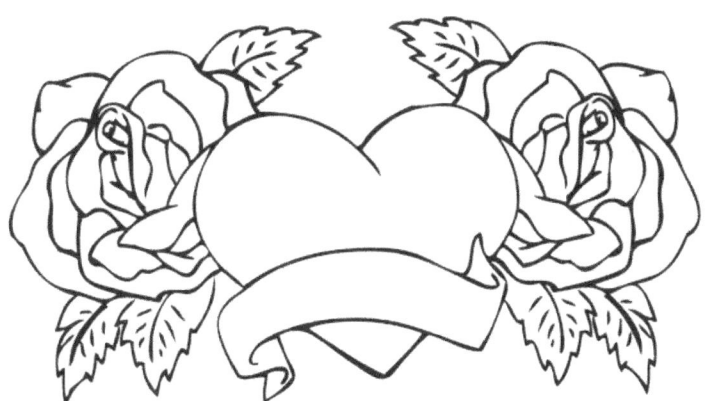

DADAMerra©

© 2020 DADAMERRA ALL RIGHTS RESERVED

NO PART OF THIS BOOK MAY BE REPRODUCED, STORED IN A RETRIEVAL SYSTEM, STORED IN A DATABASE AND / OR PUBLISHED IN ANY FORM OR BY ANY MEANS, ELECTRONIC, MECHANICAL, PHOTOCOPYING, RECORDING OR OTHERWISE, WITHOUT THE PRIOR WRITTEN PERMISSION OF THE PUBLISHER.

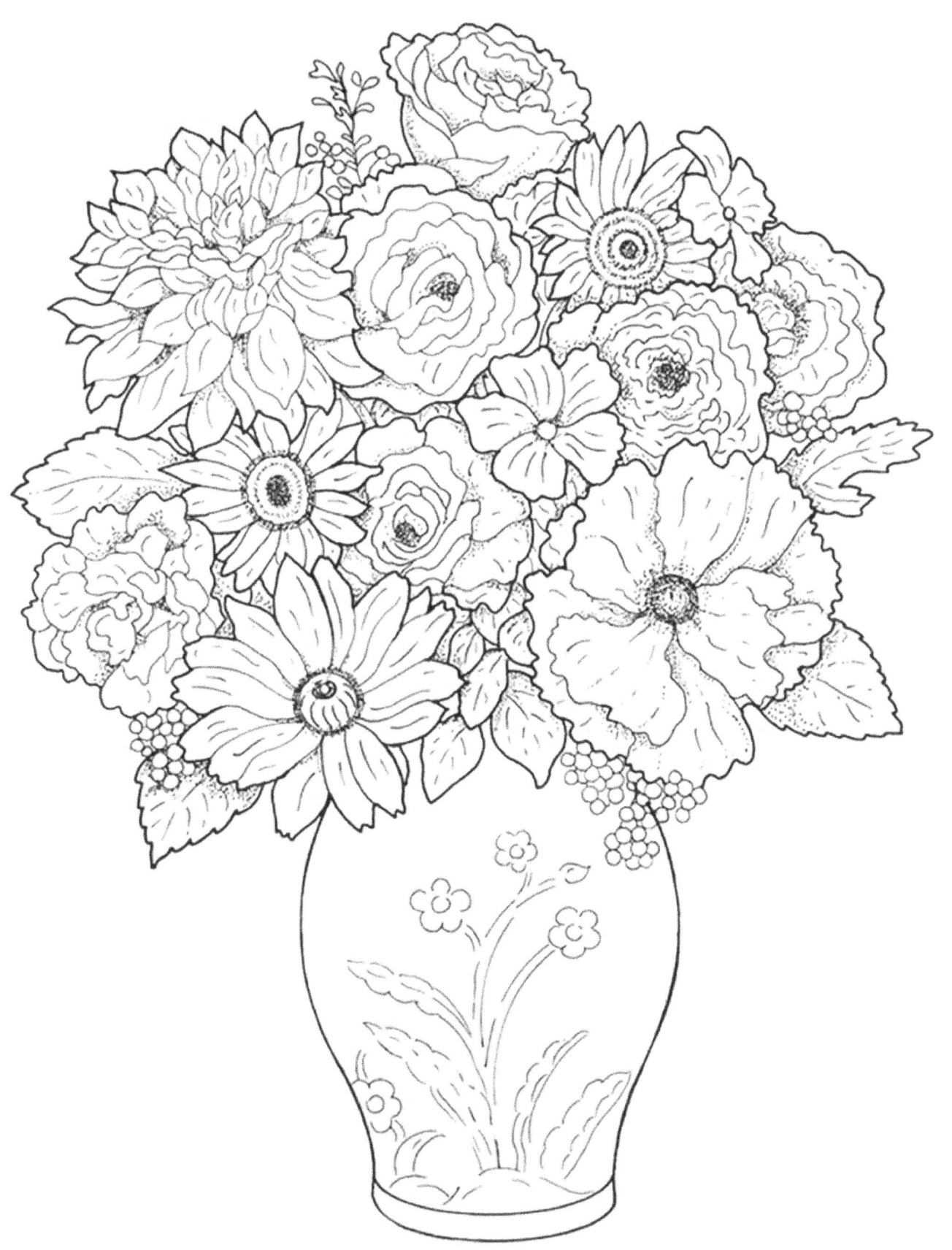

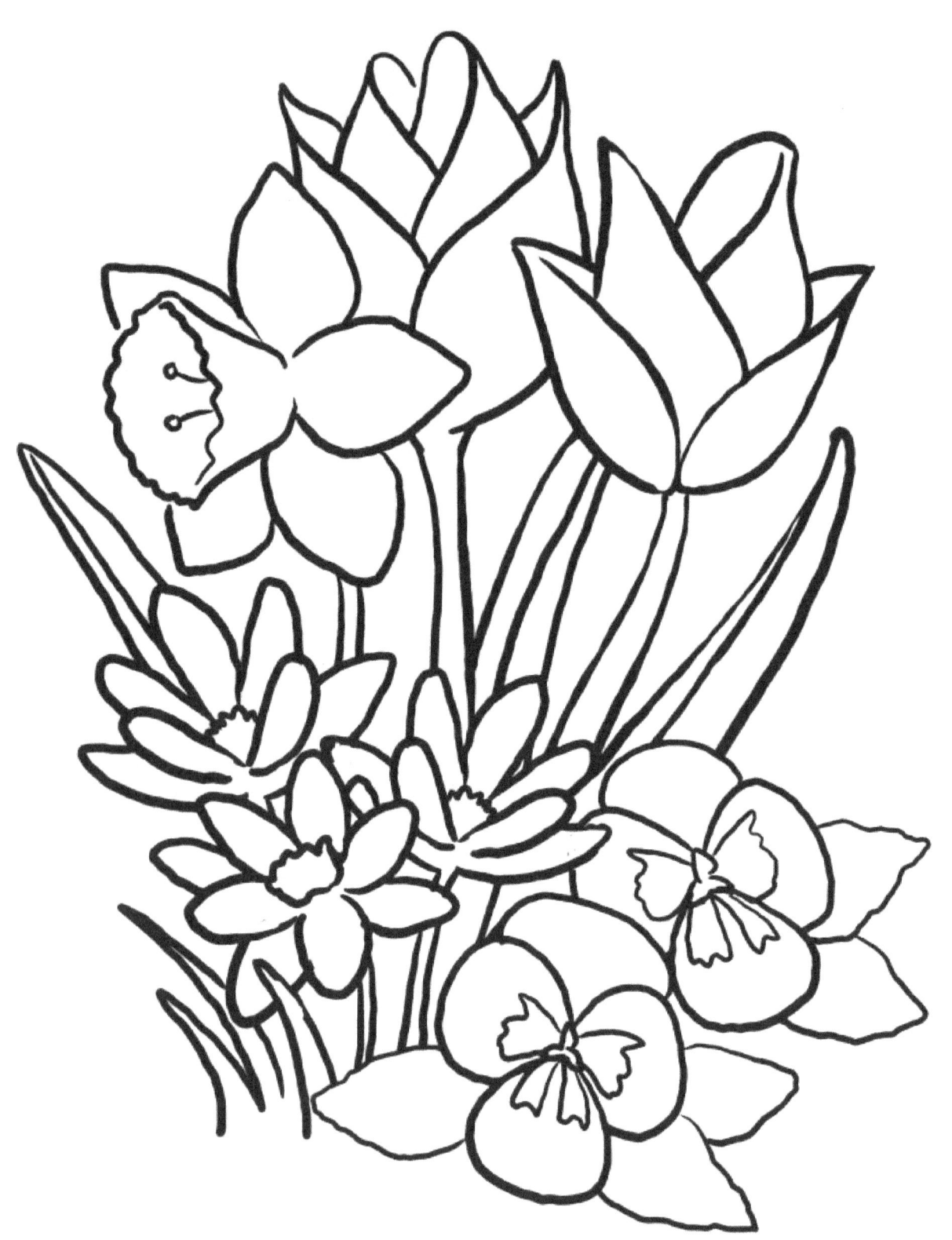

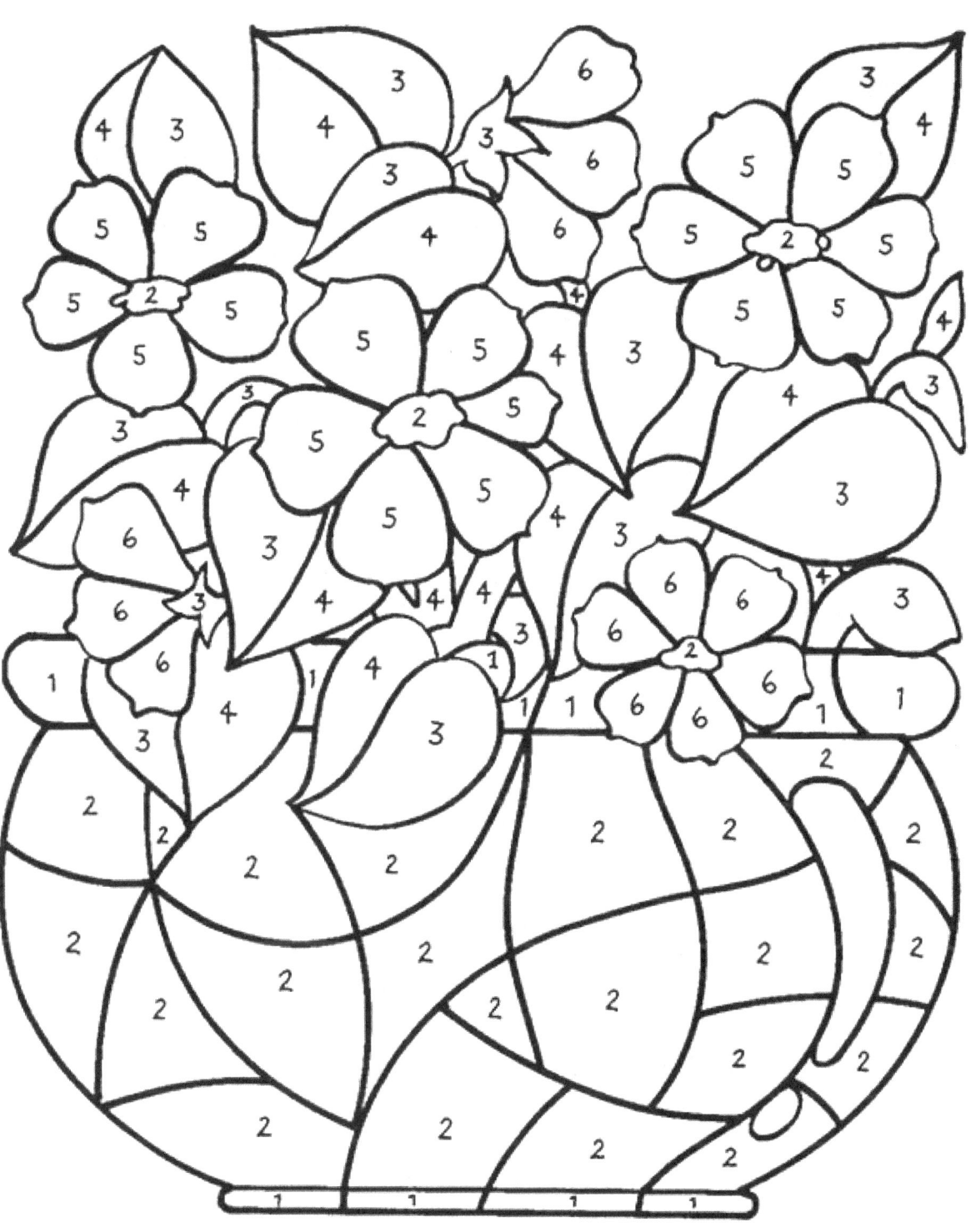

1. Red 2. Yellow 3. Light Green 4. Dark Green 5. Blue 6. Purple

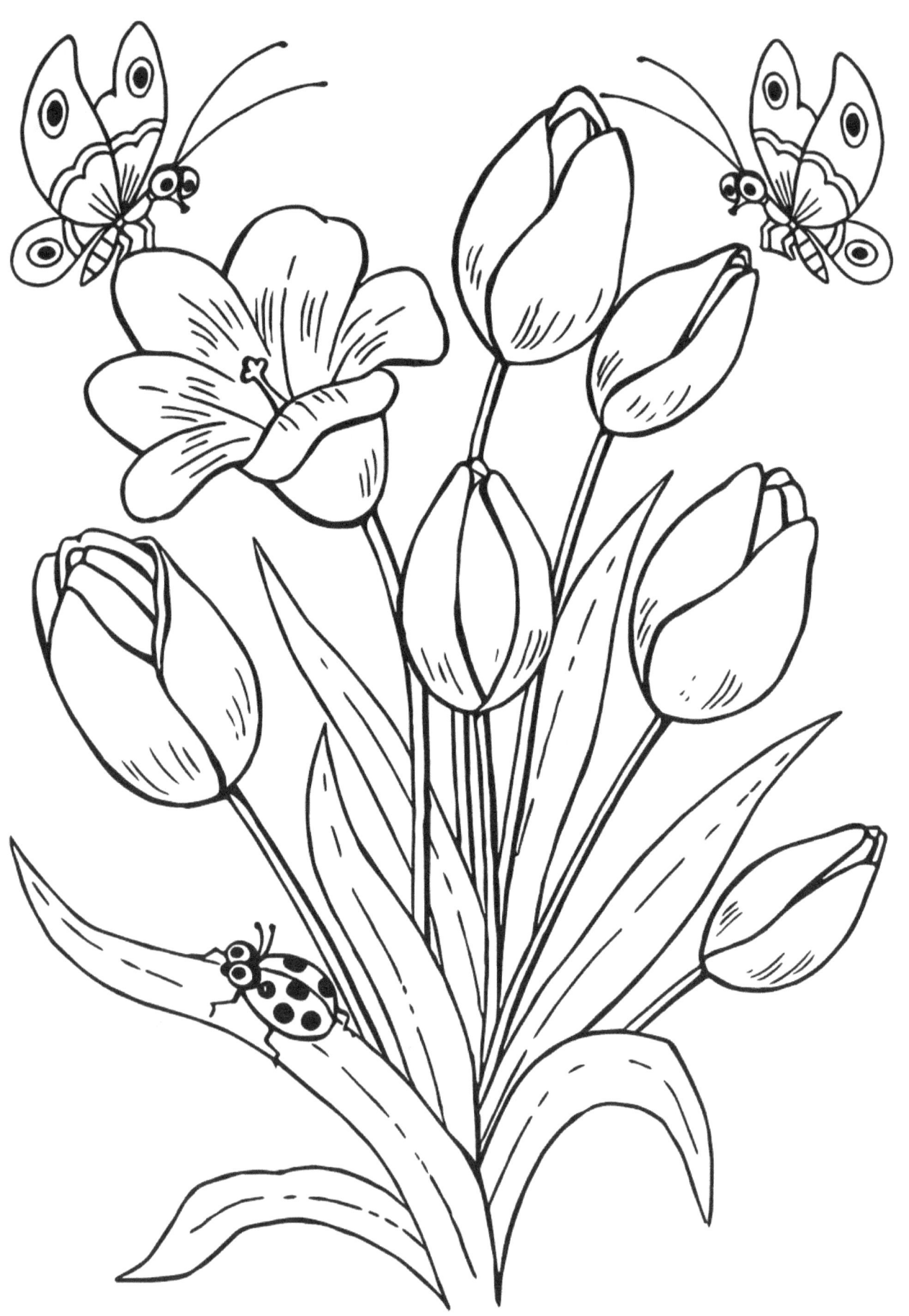

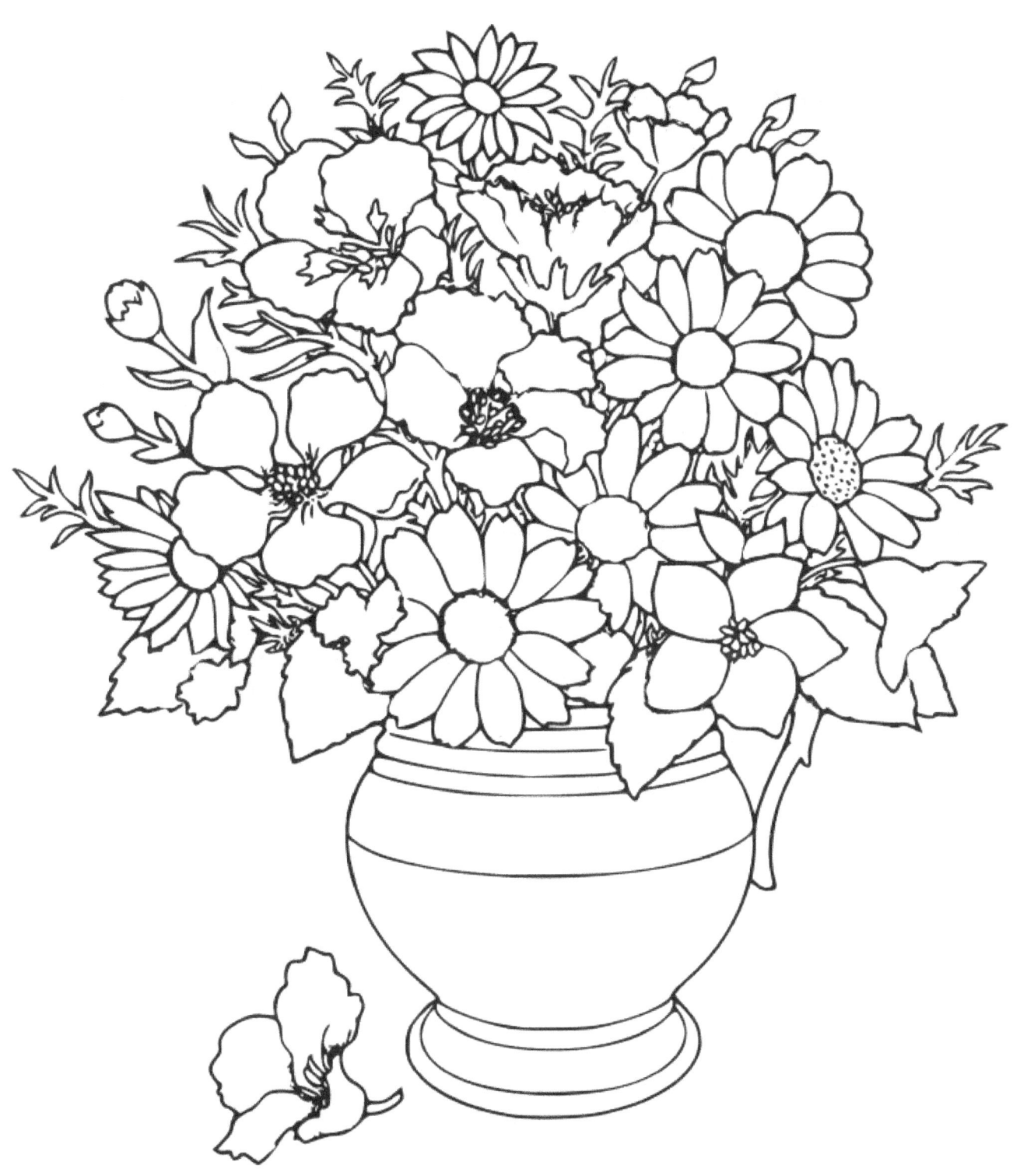

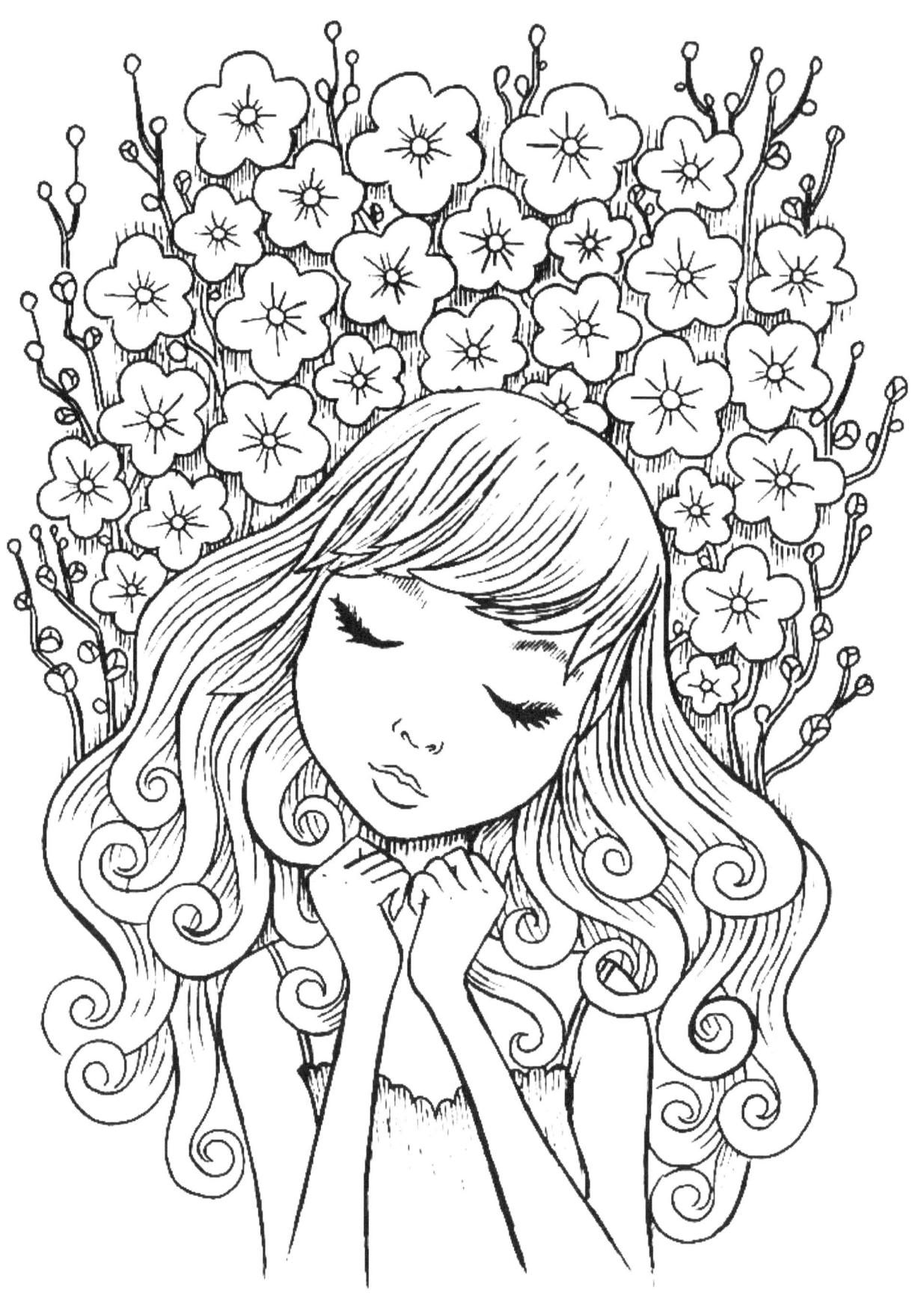

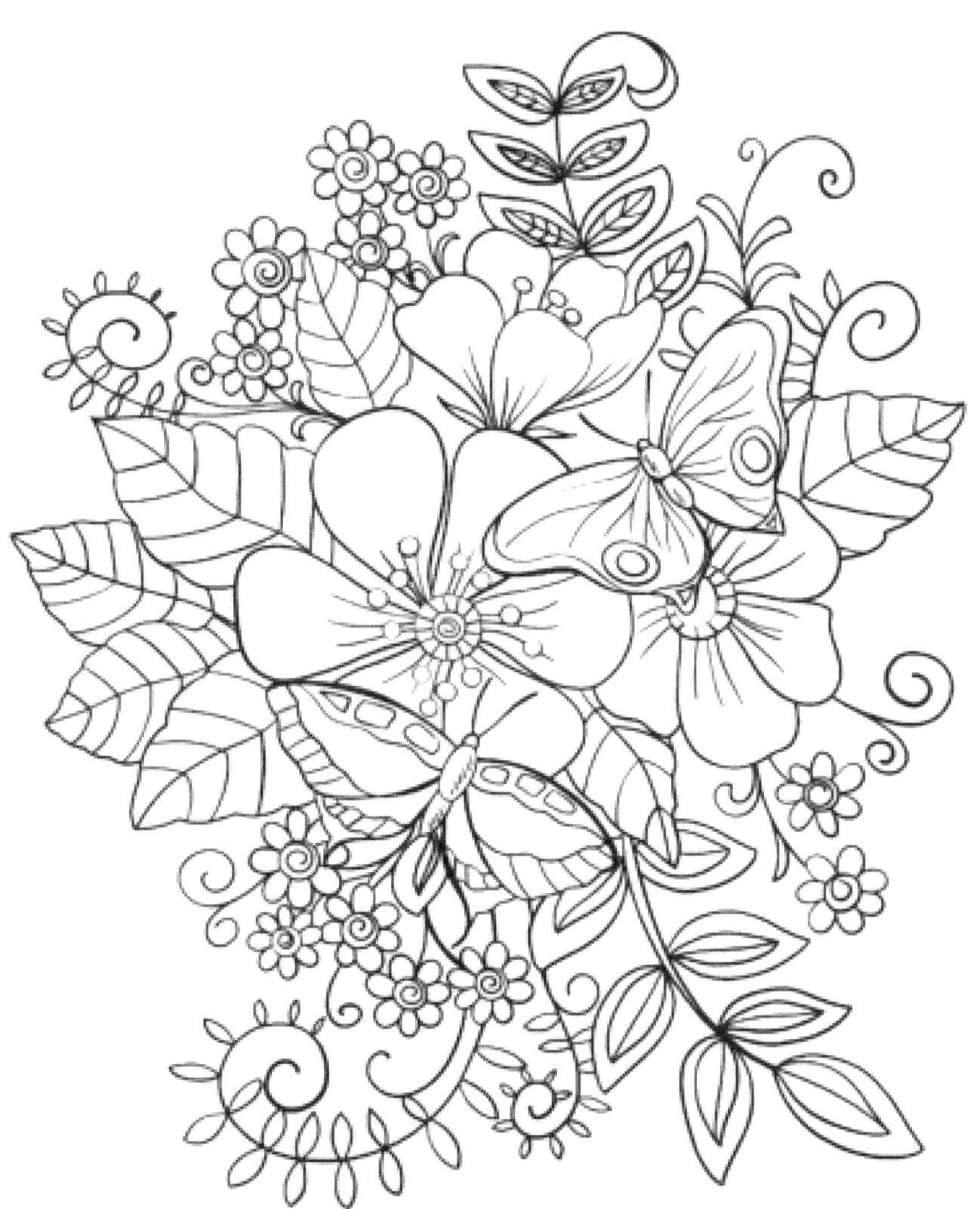

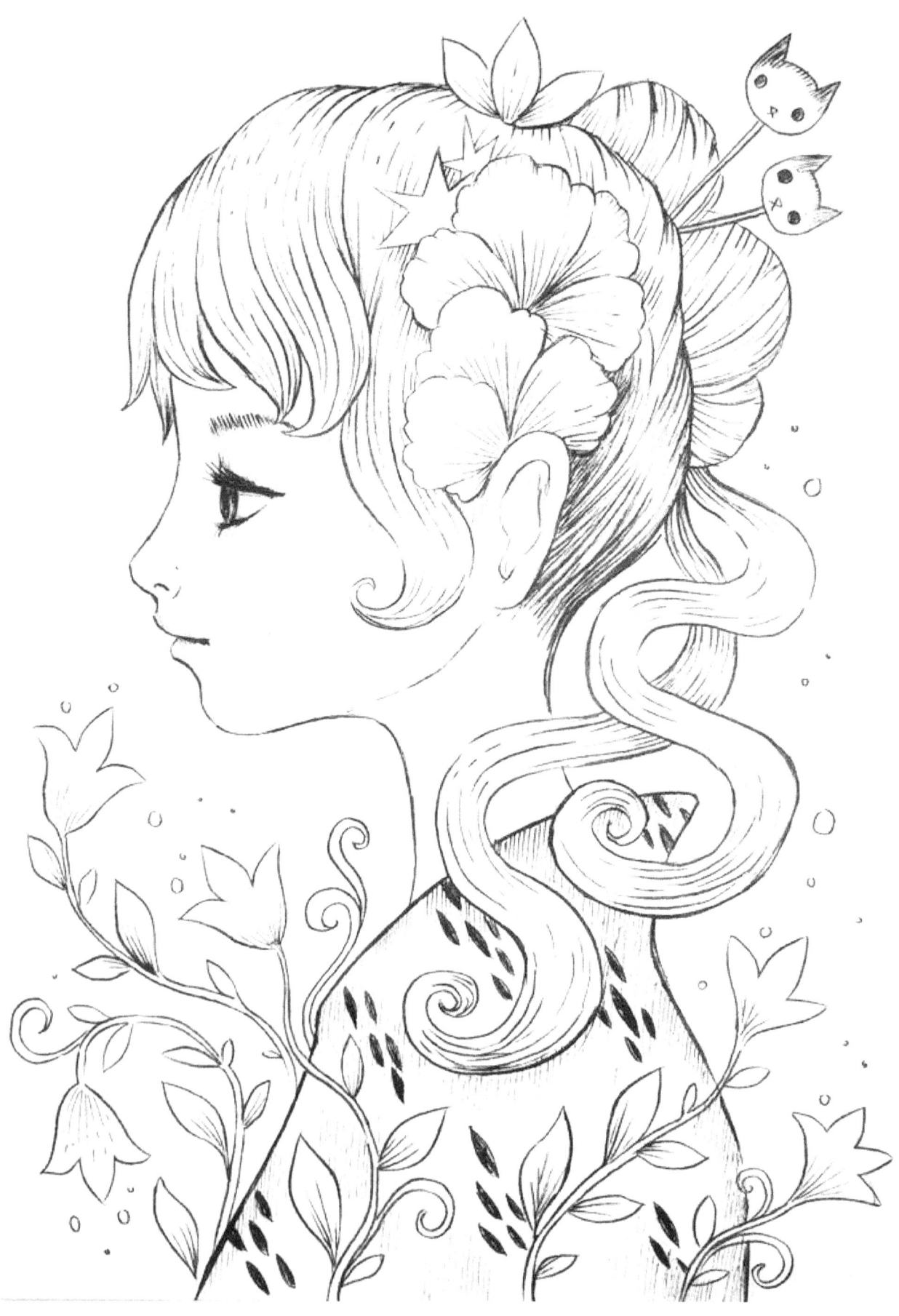

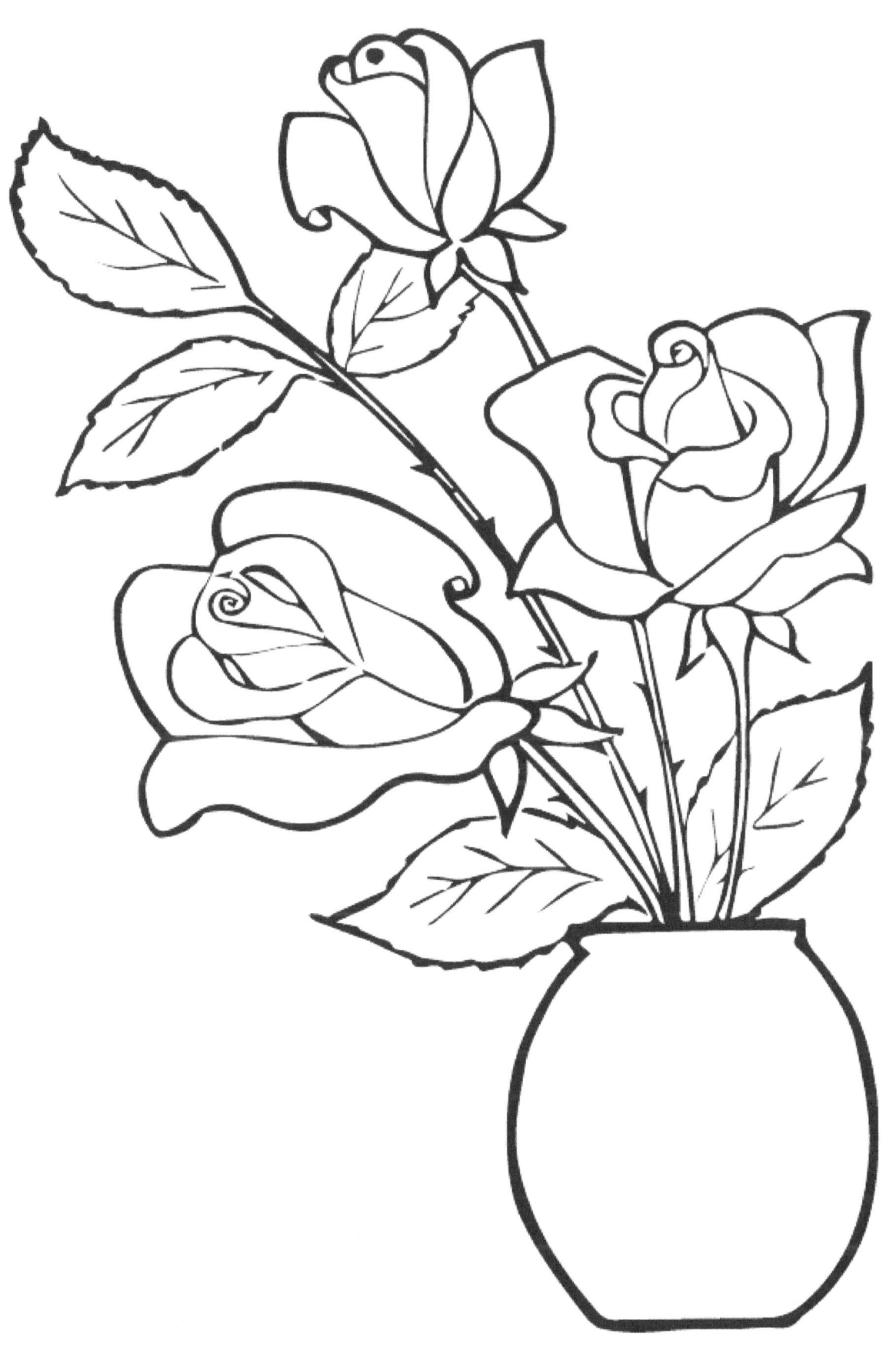

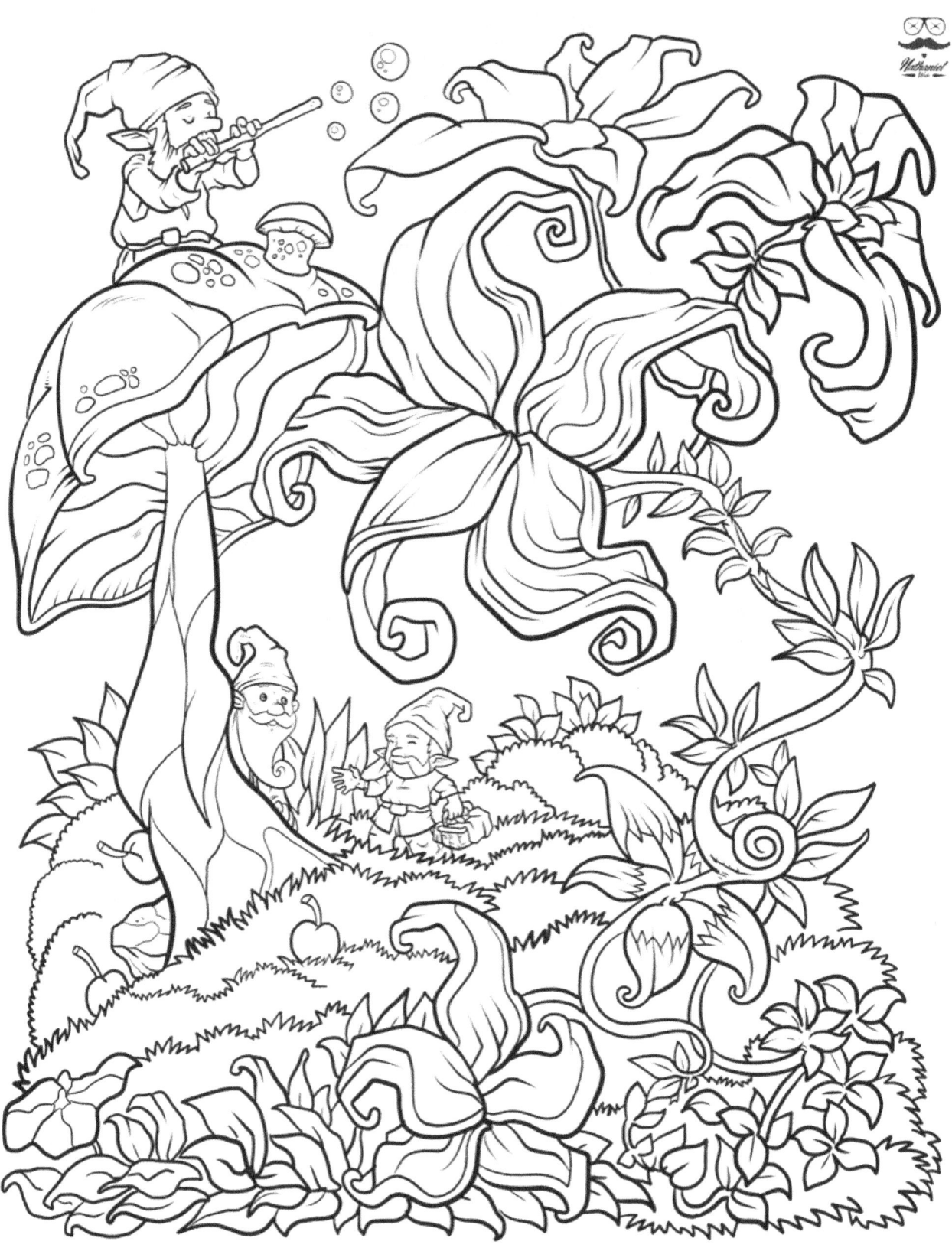

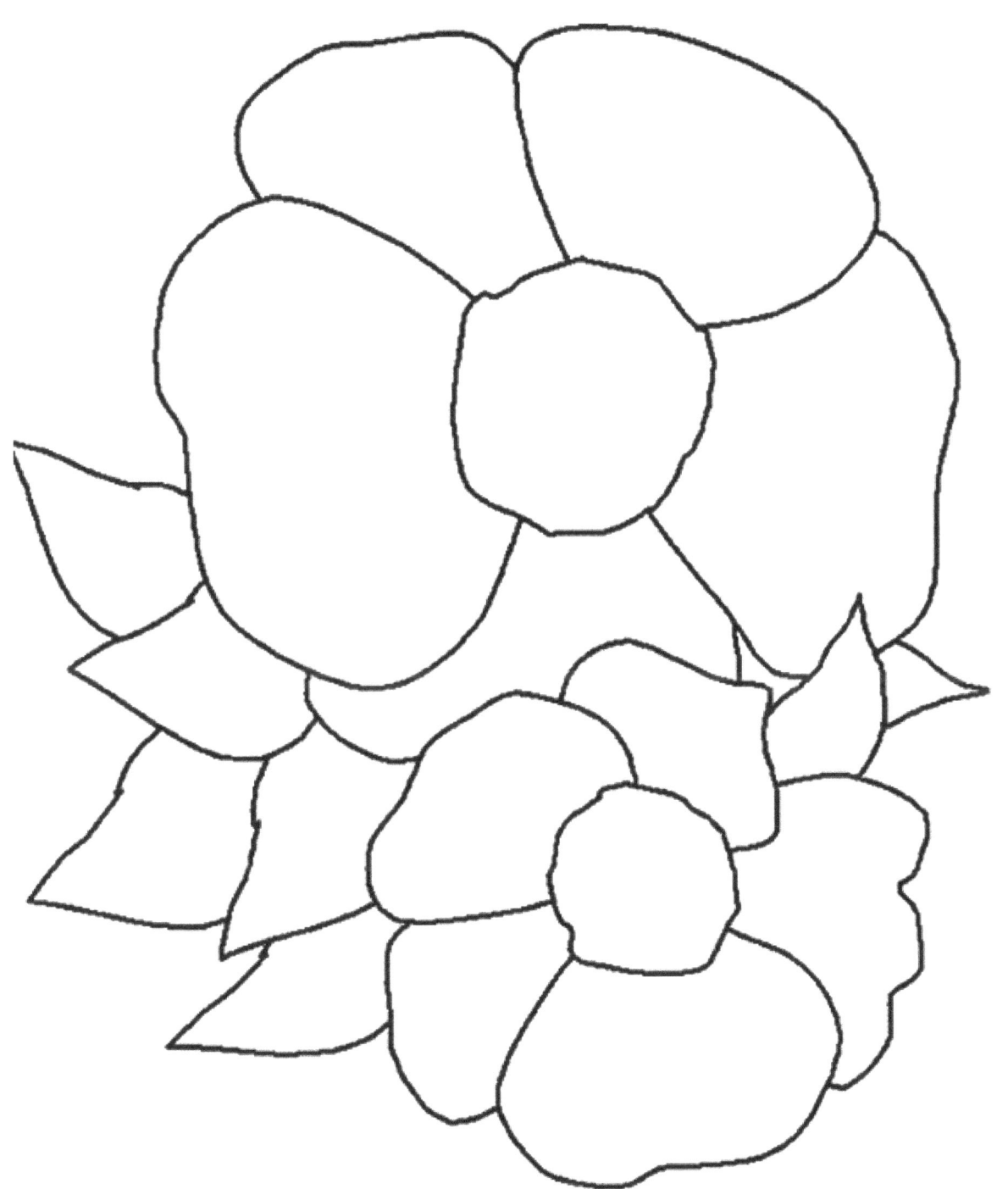

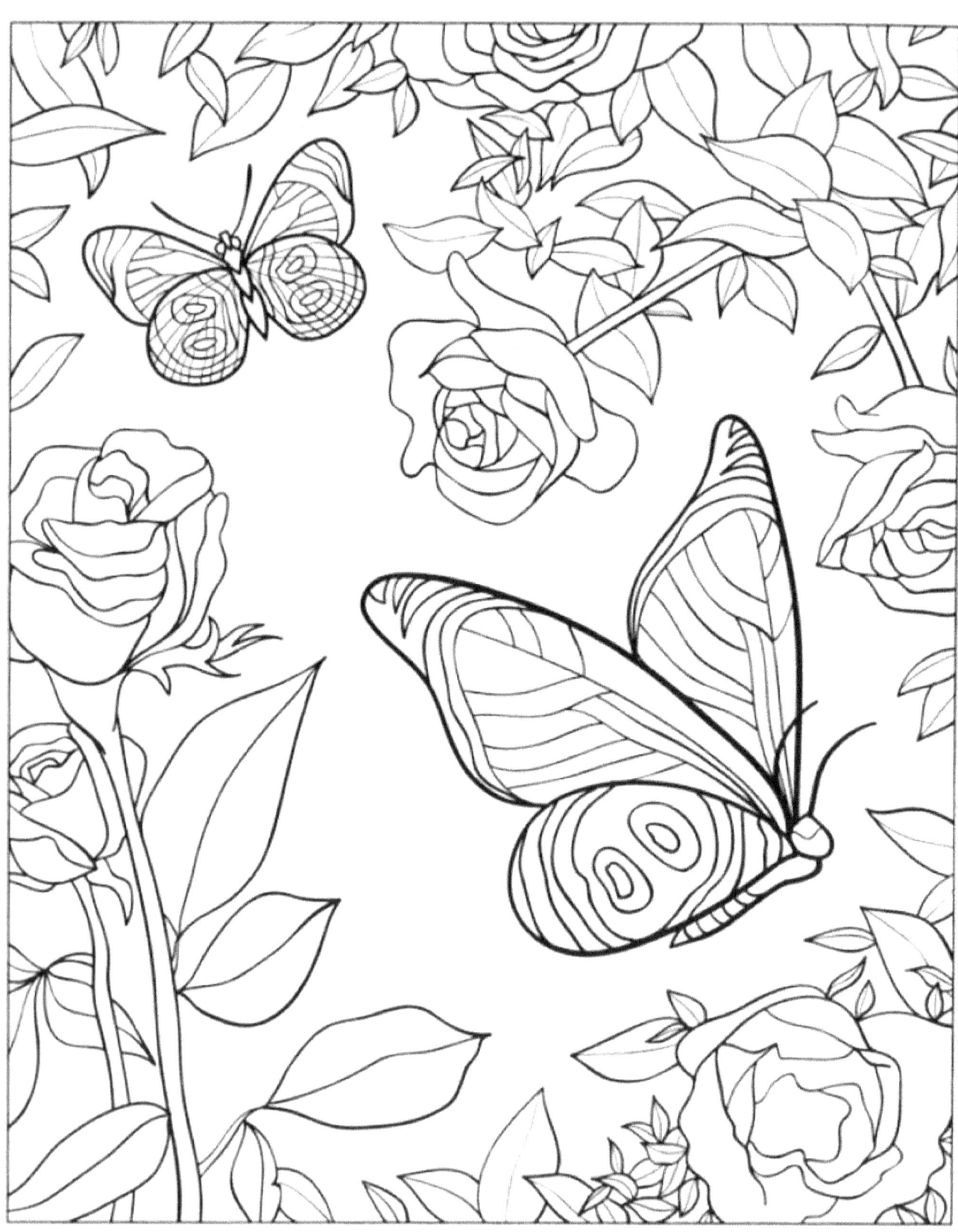

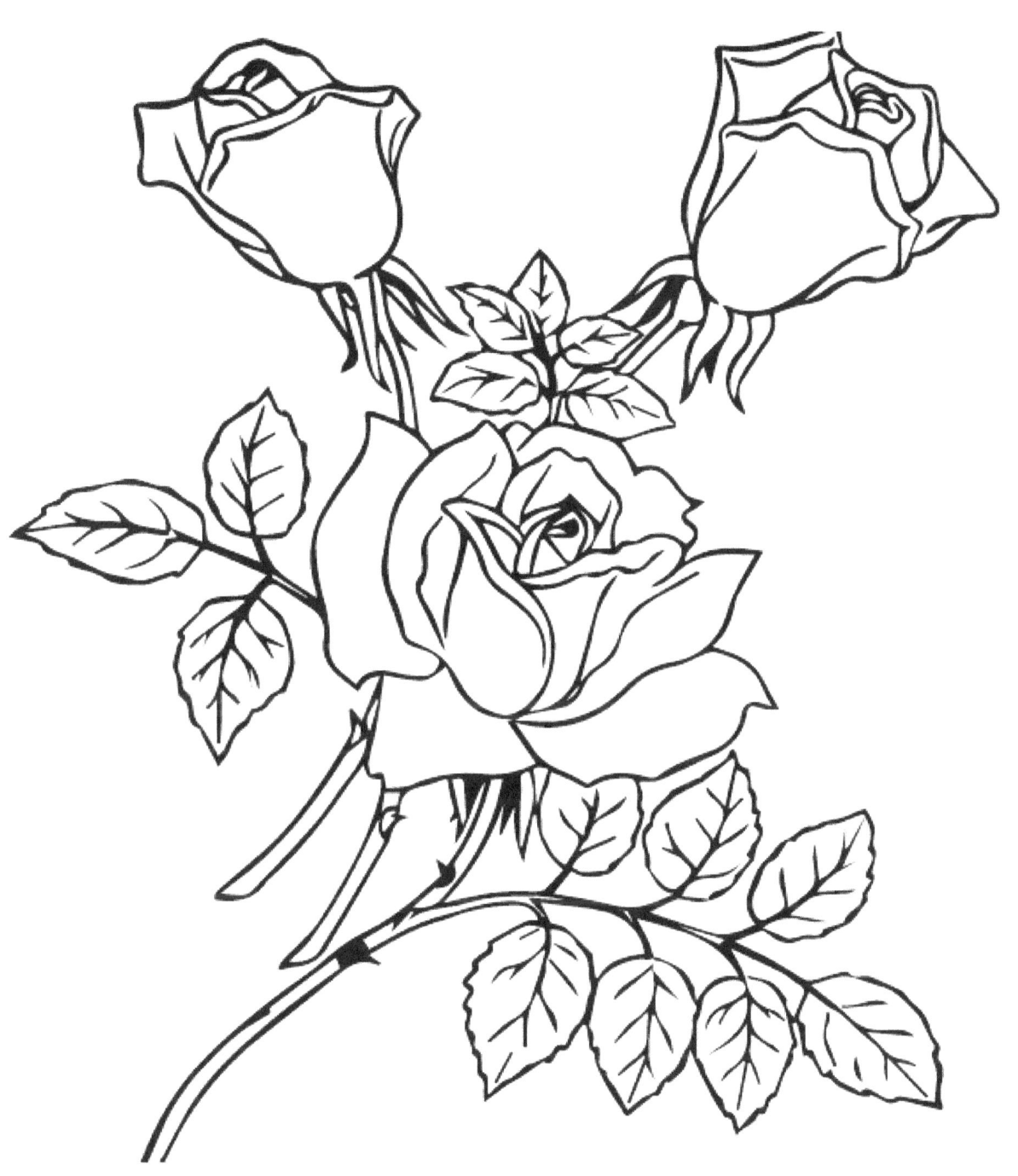

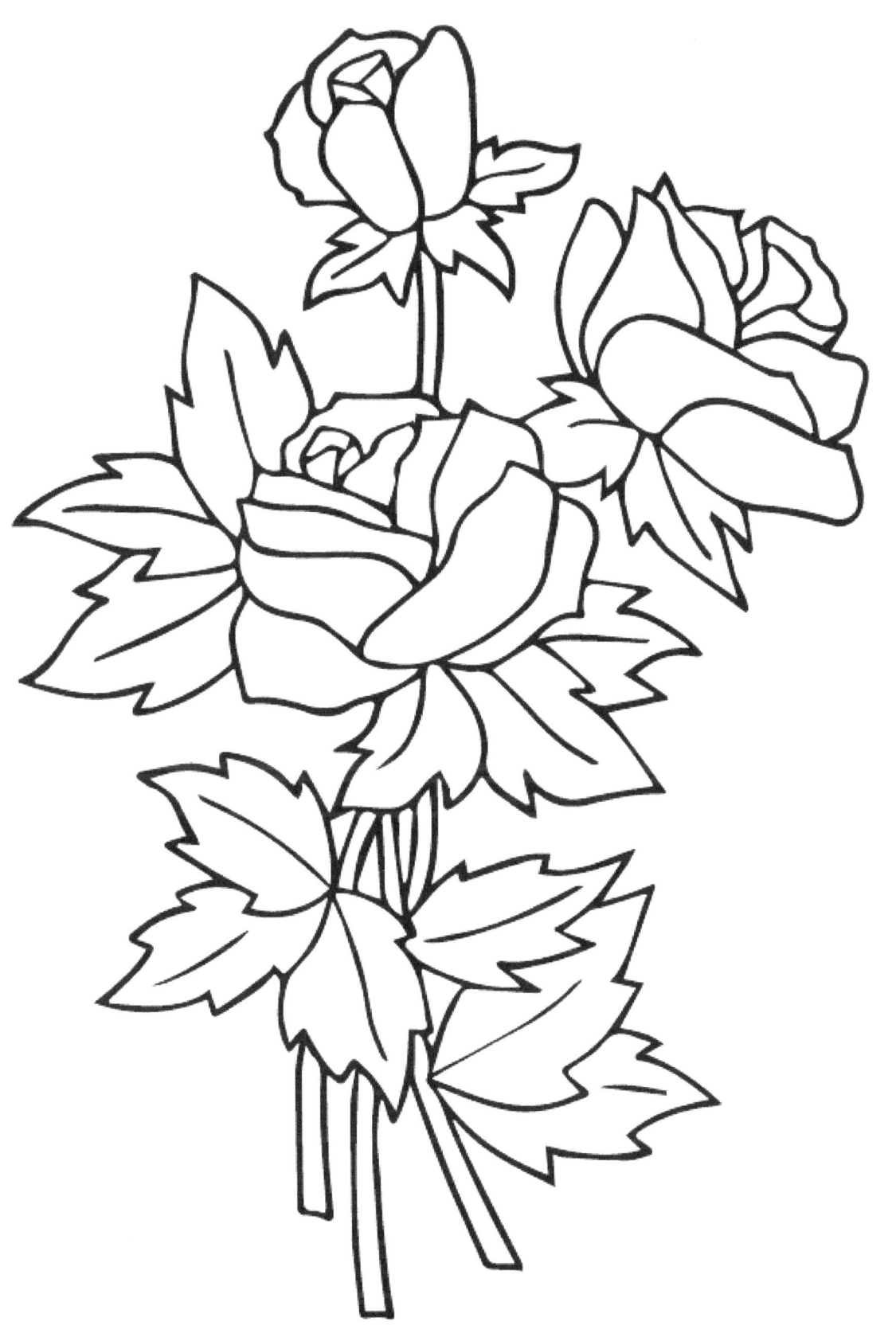

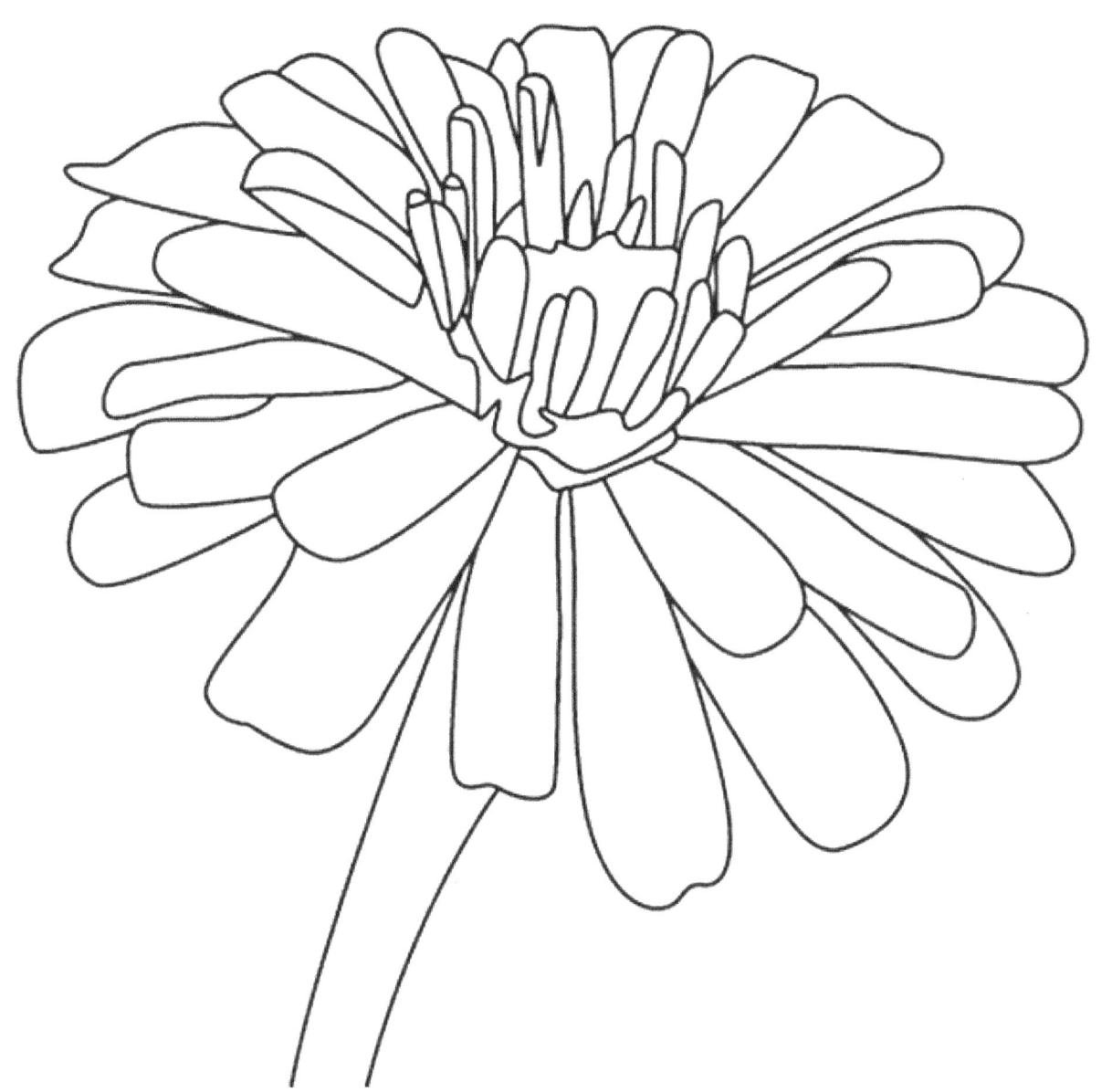

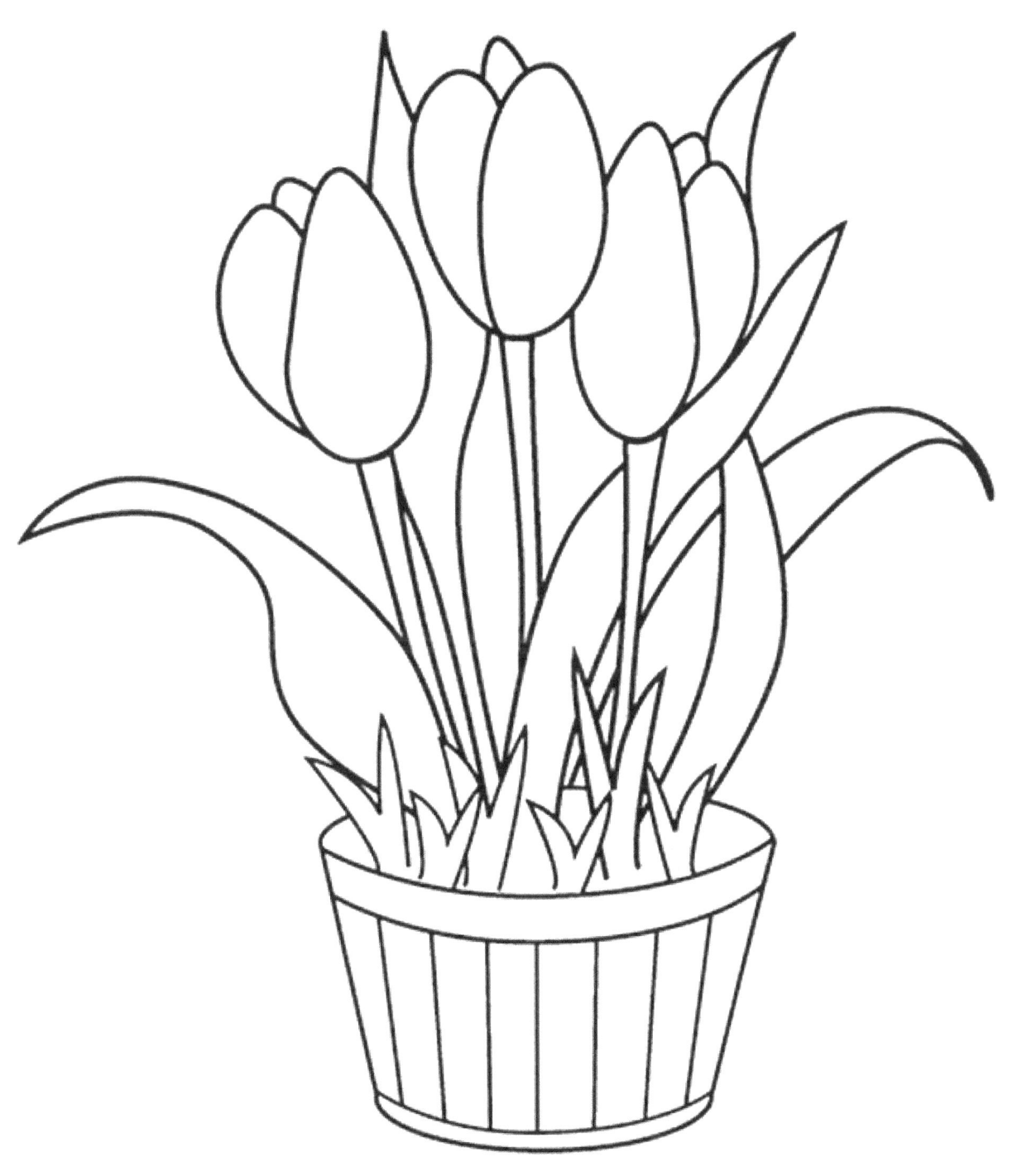

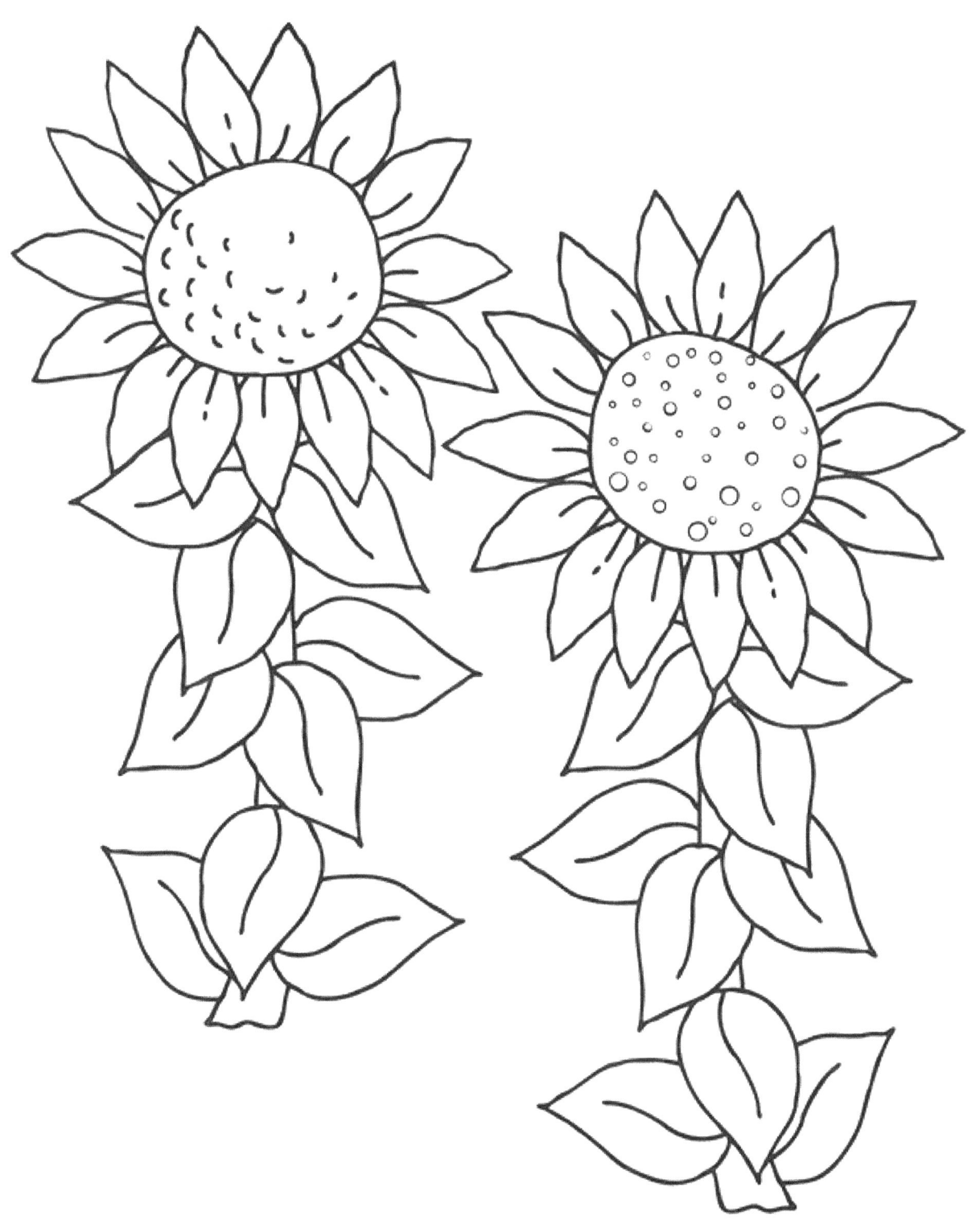

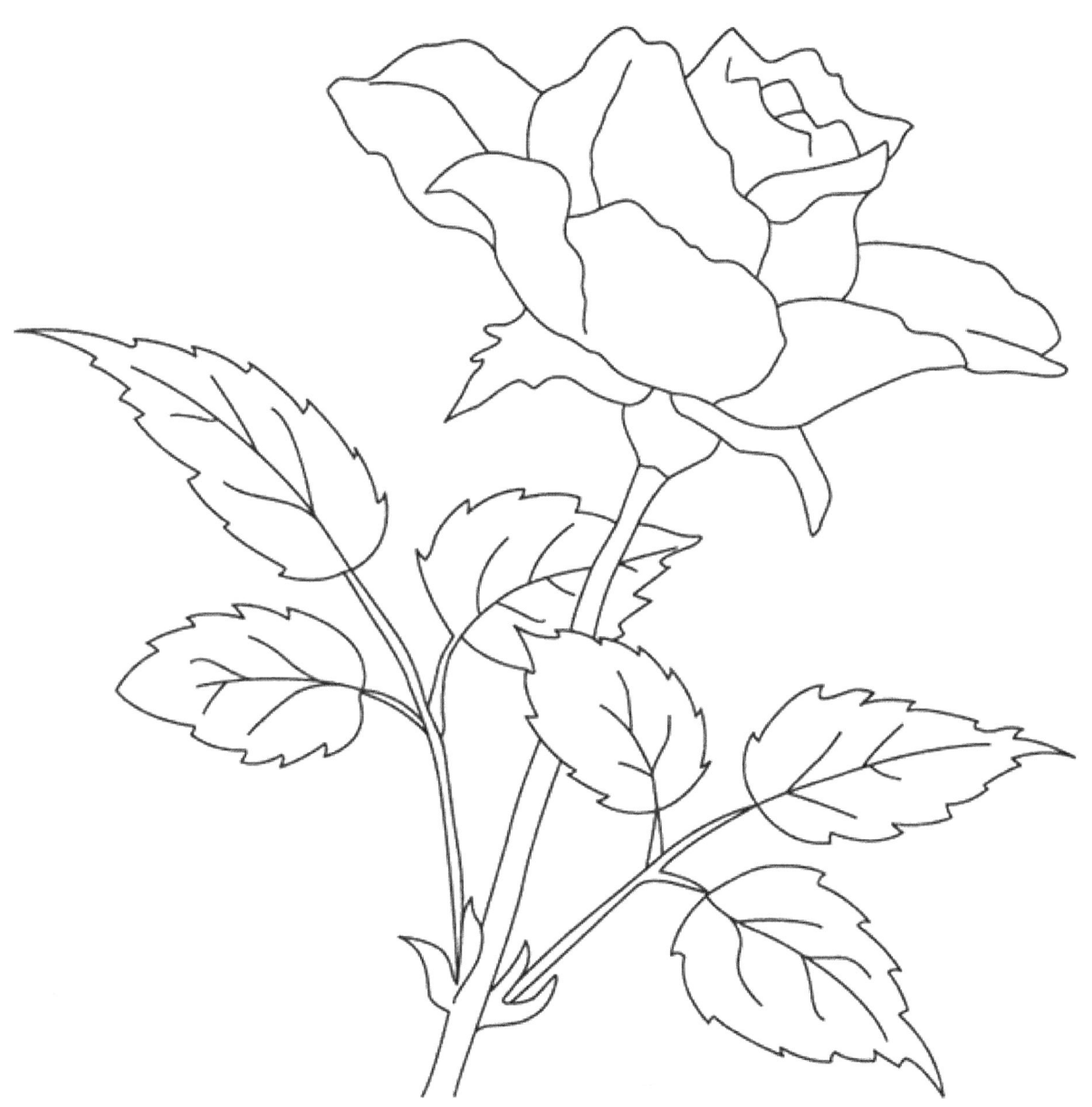

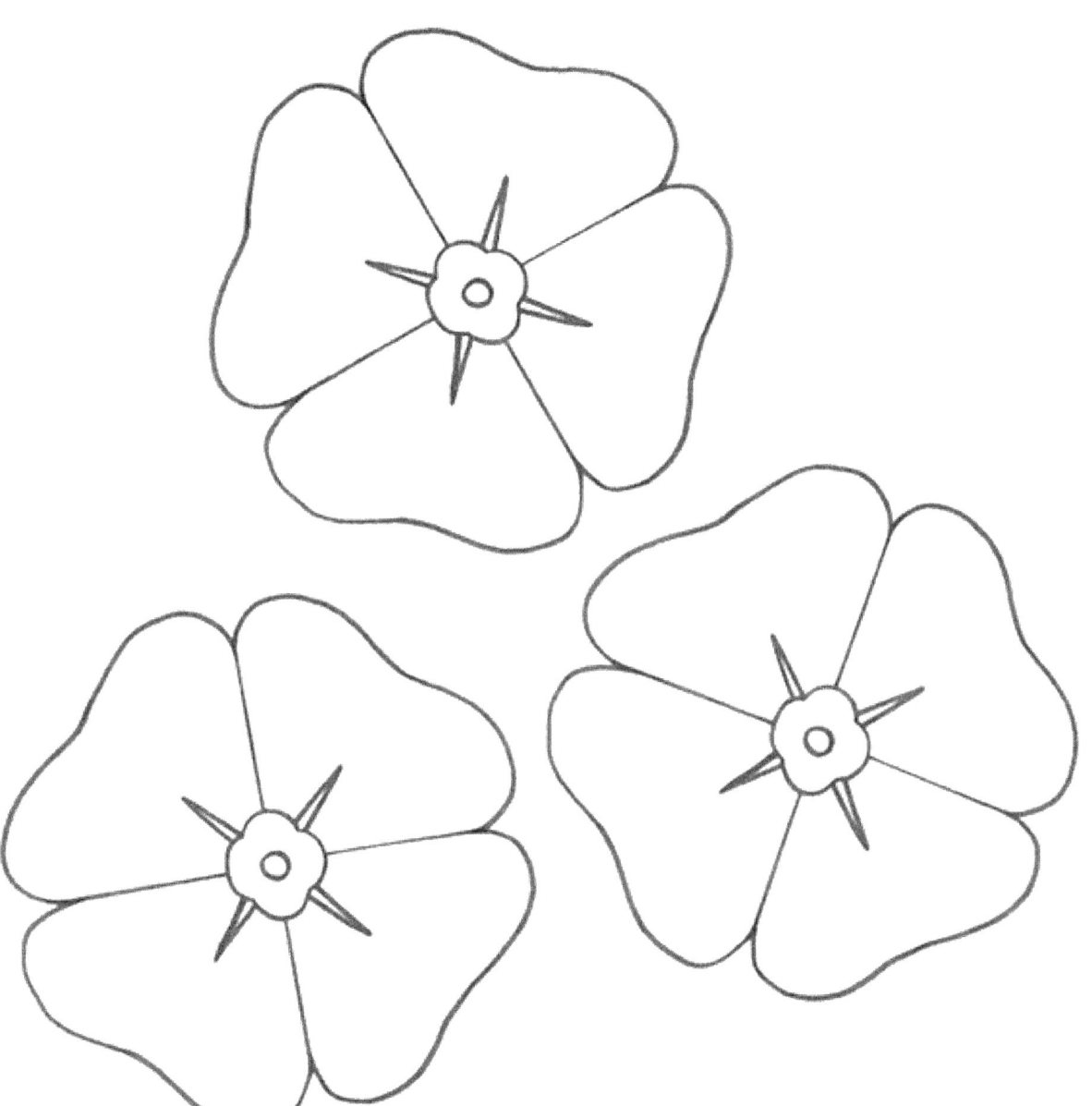

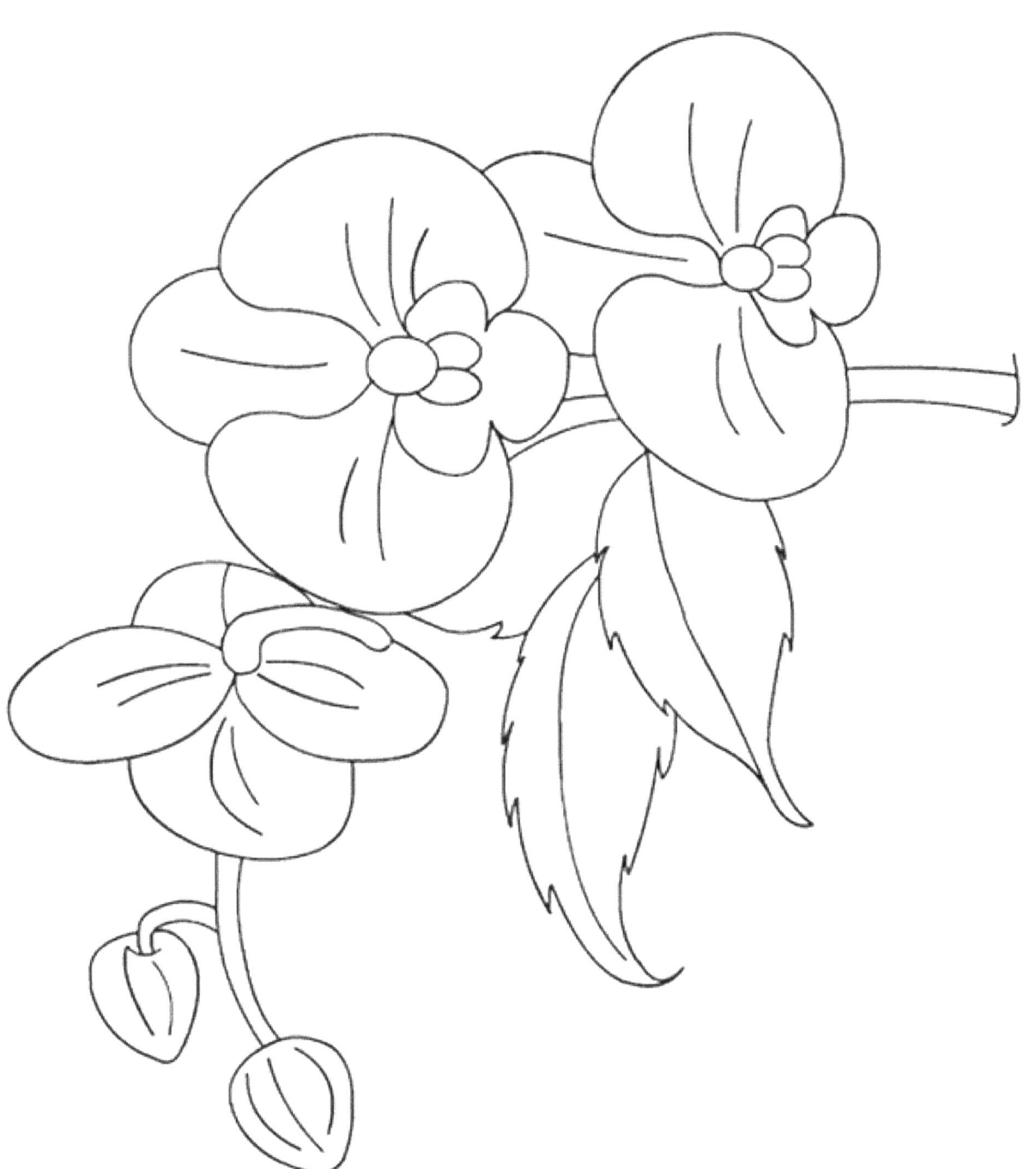

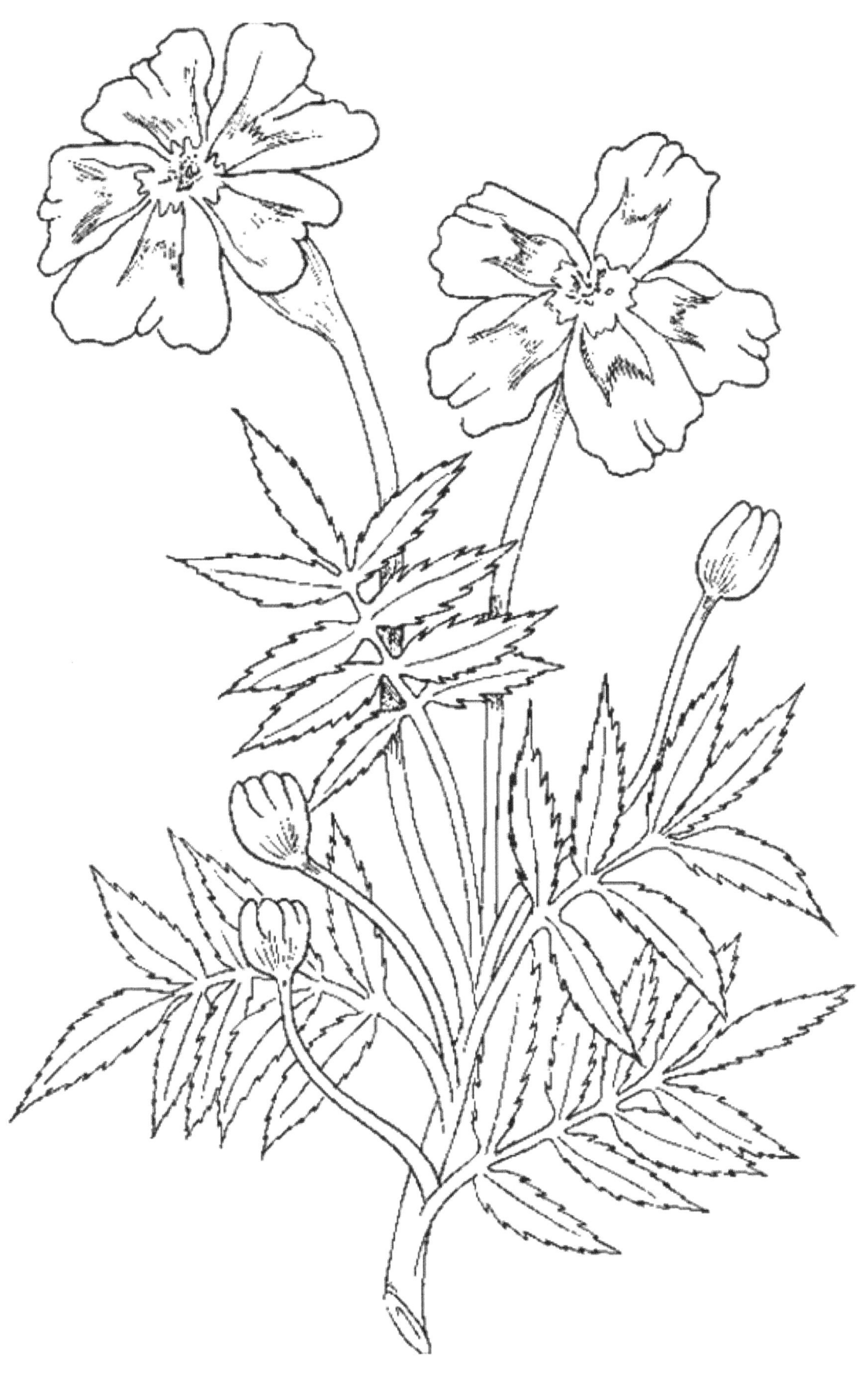

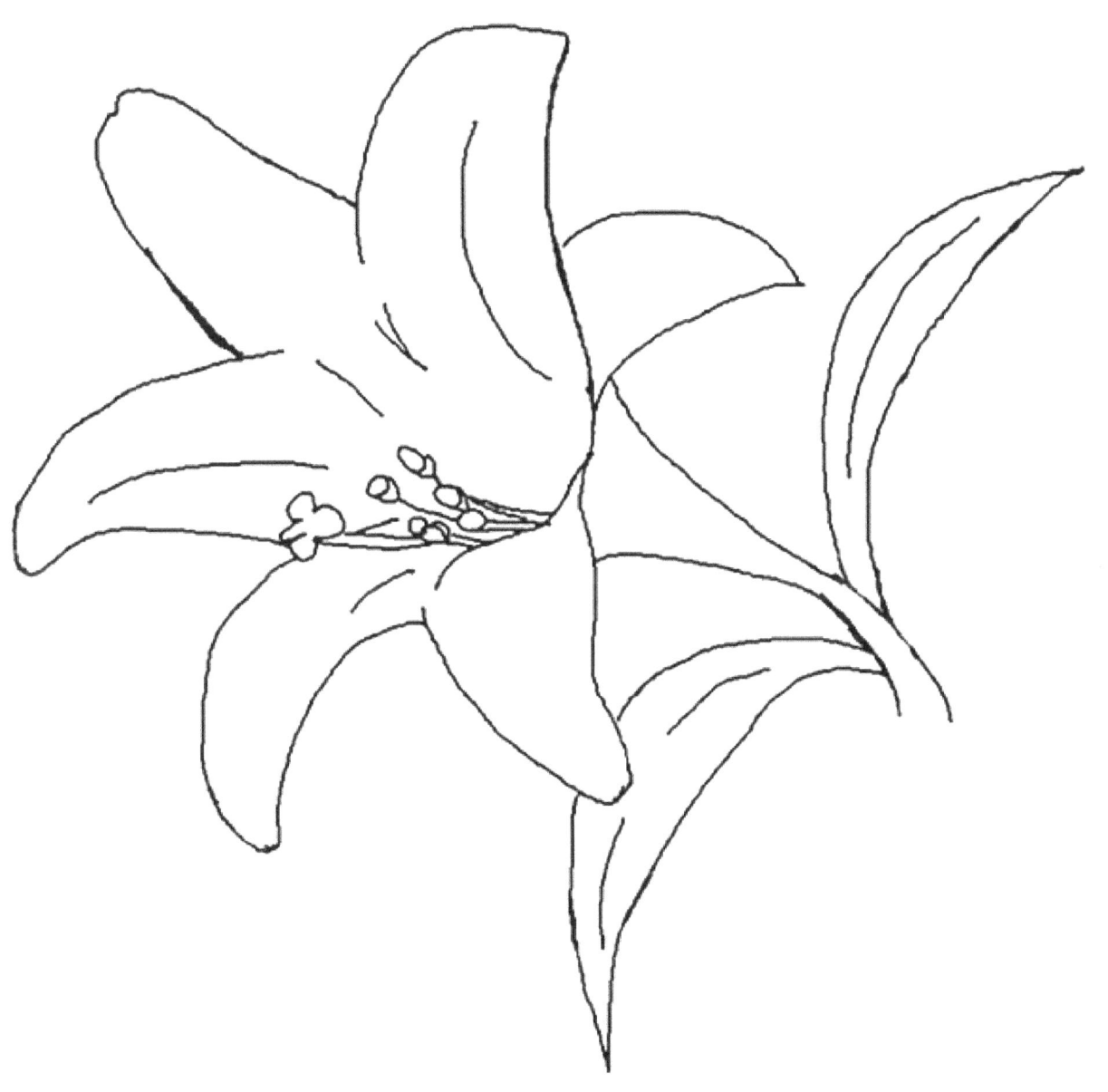

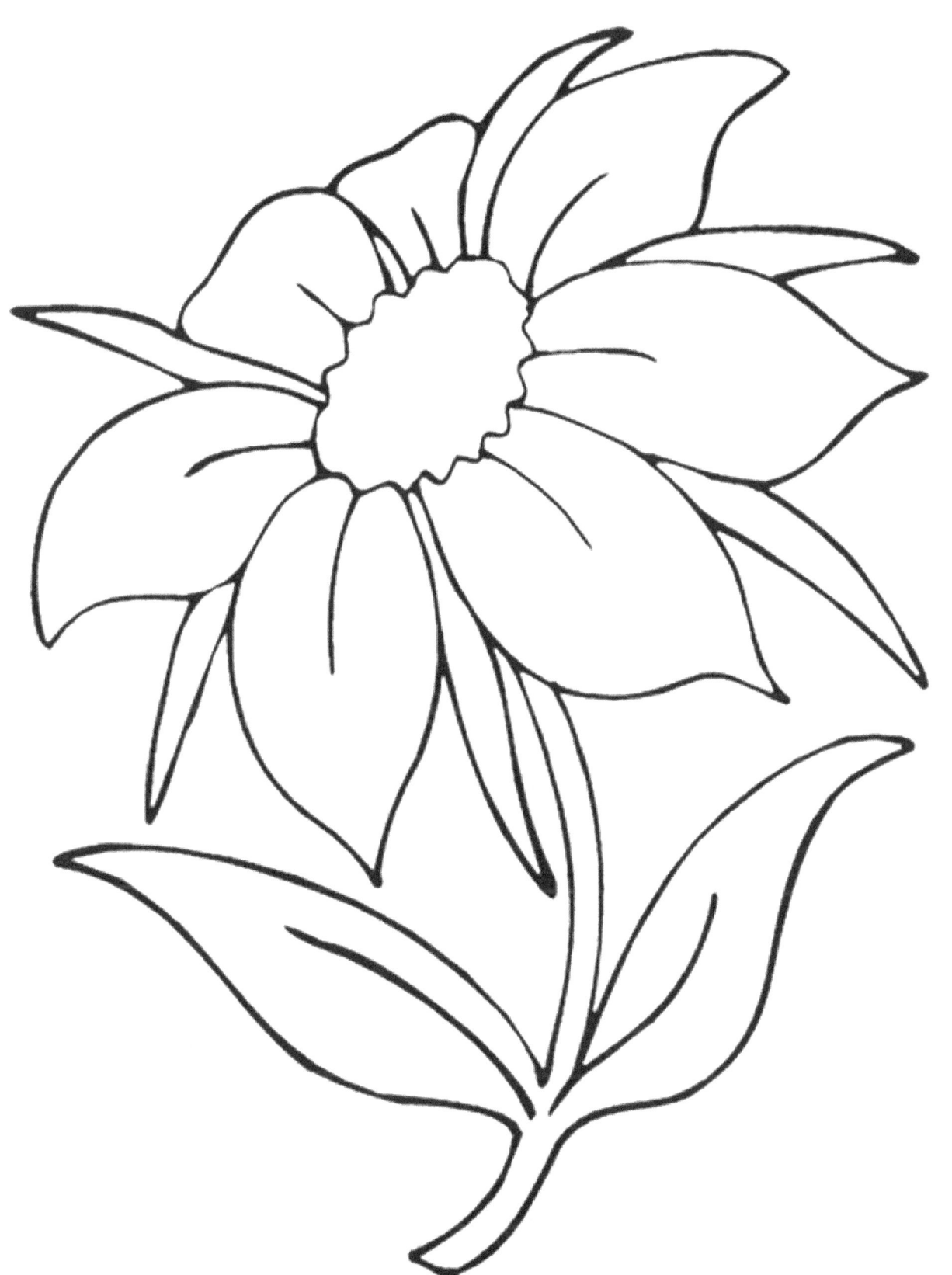

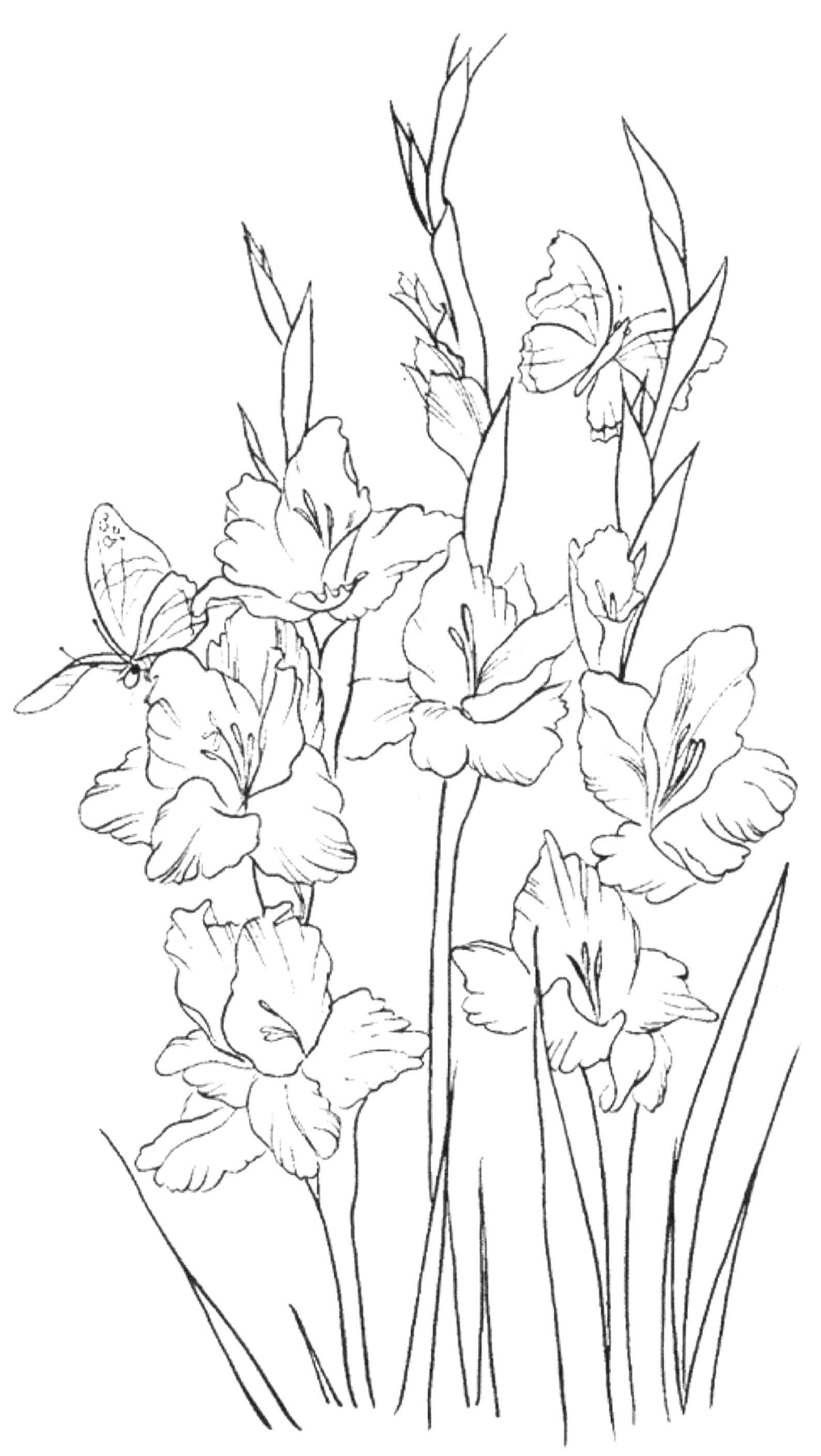

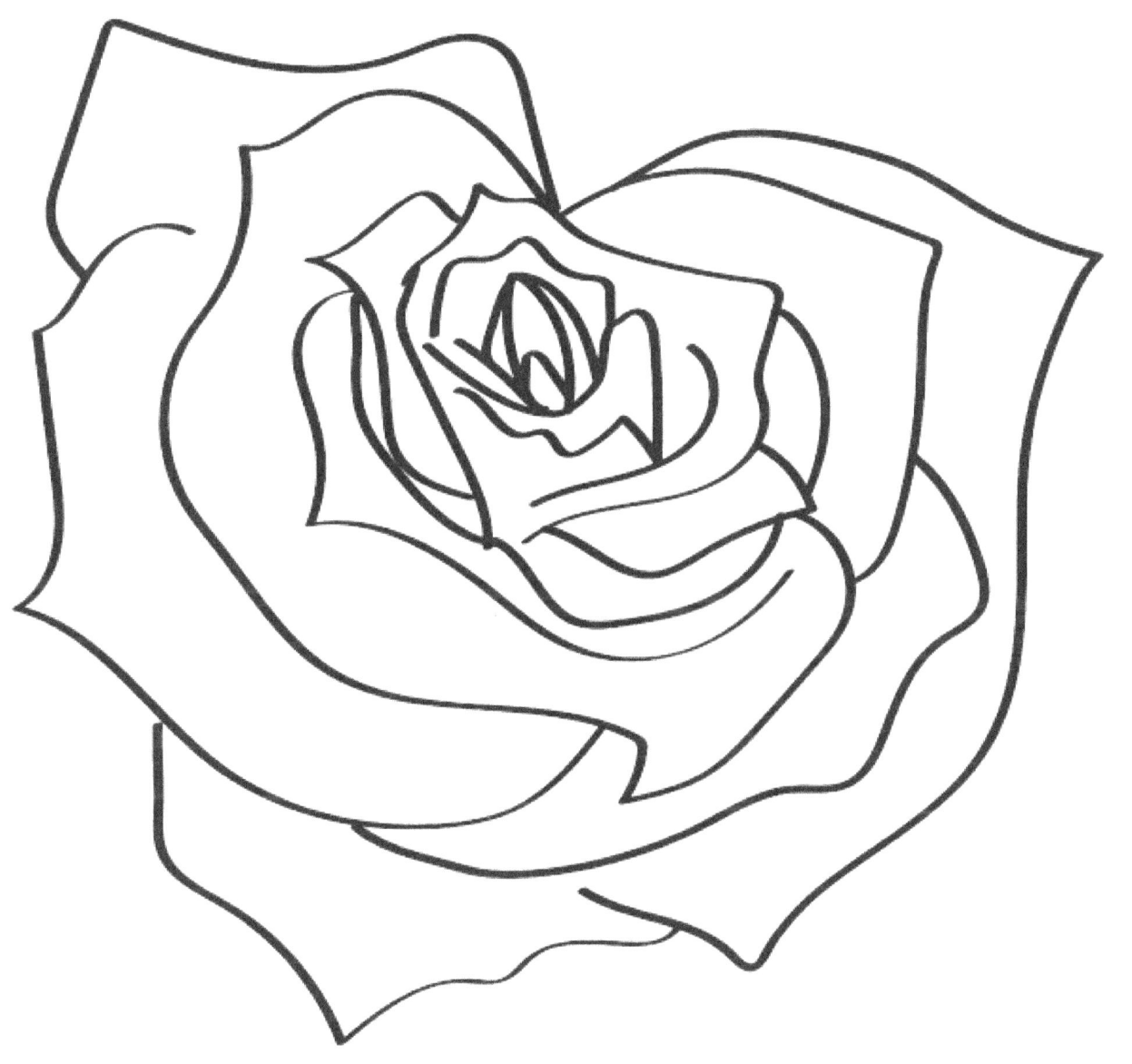

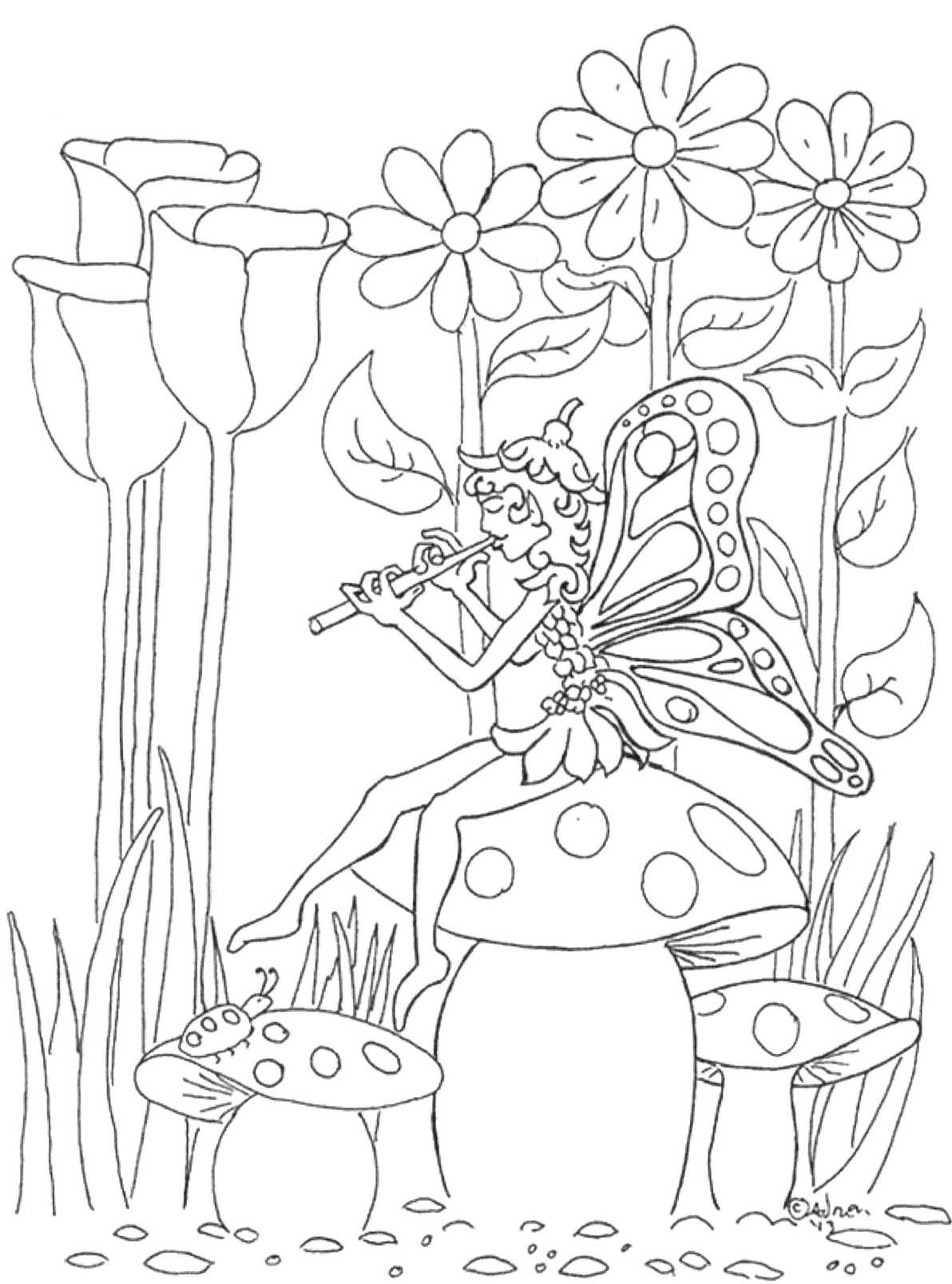

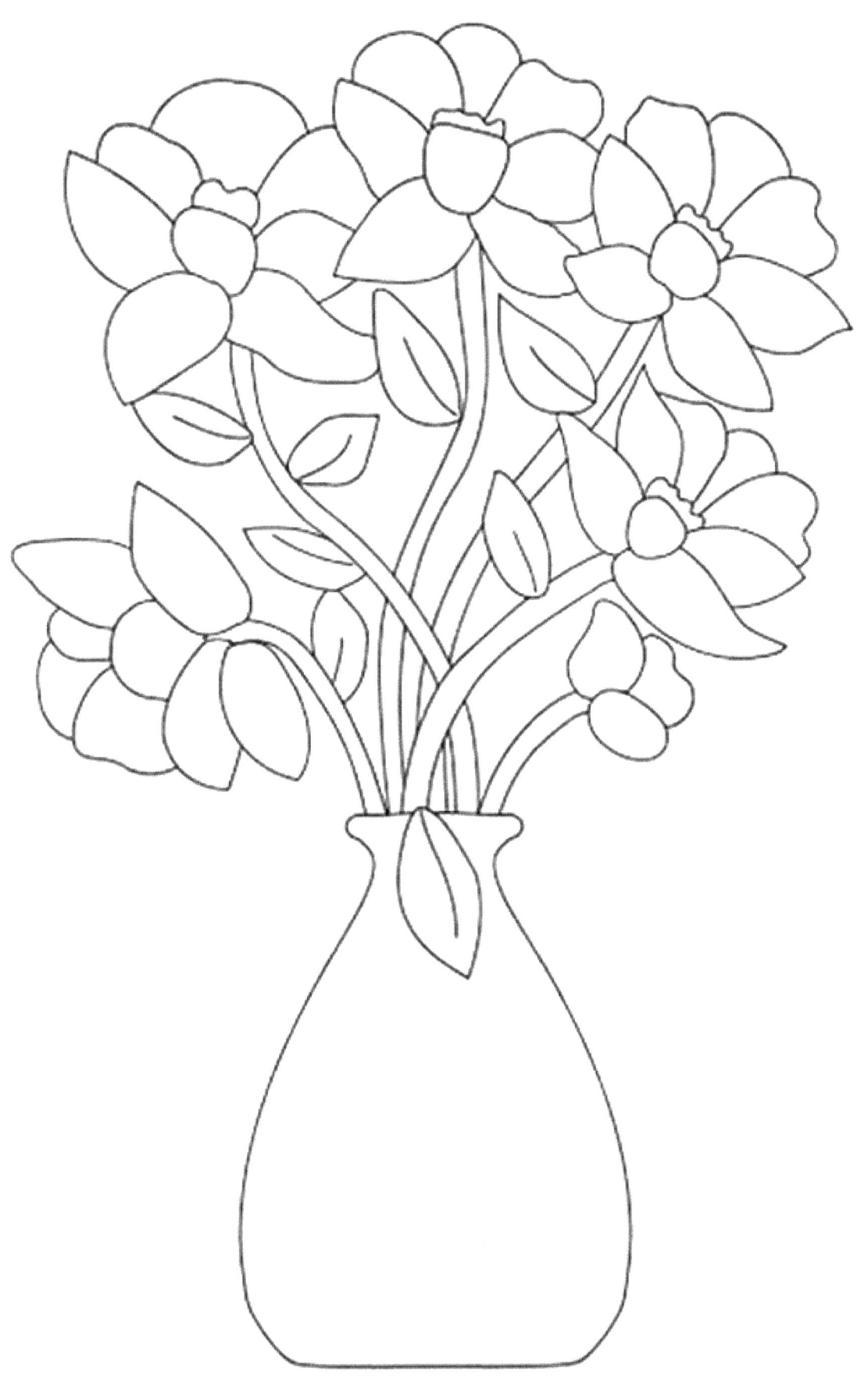

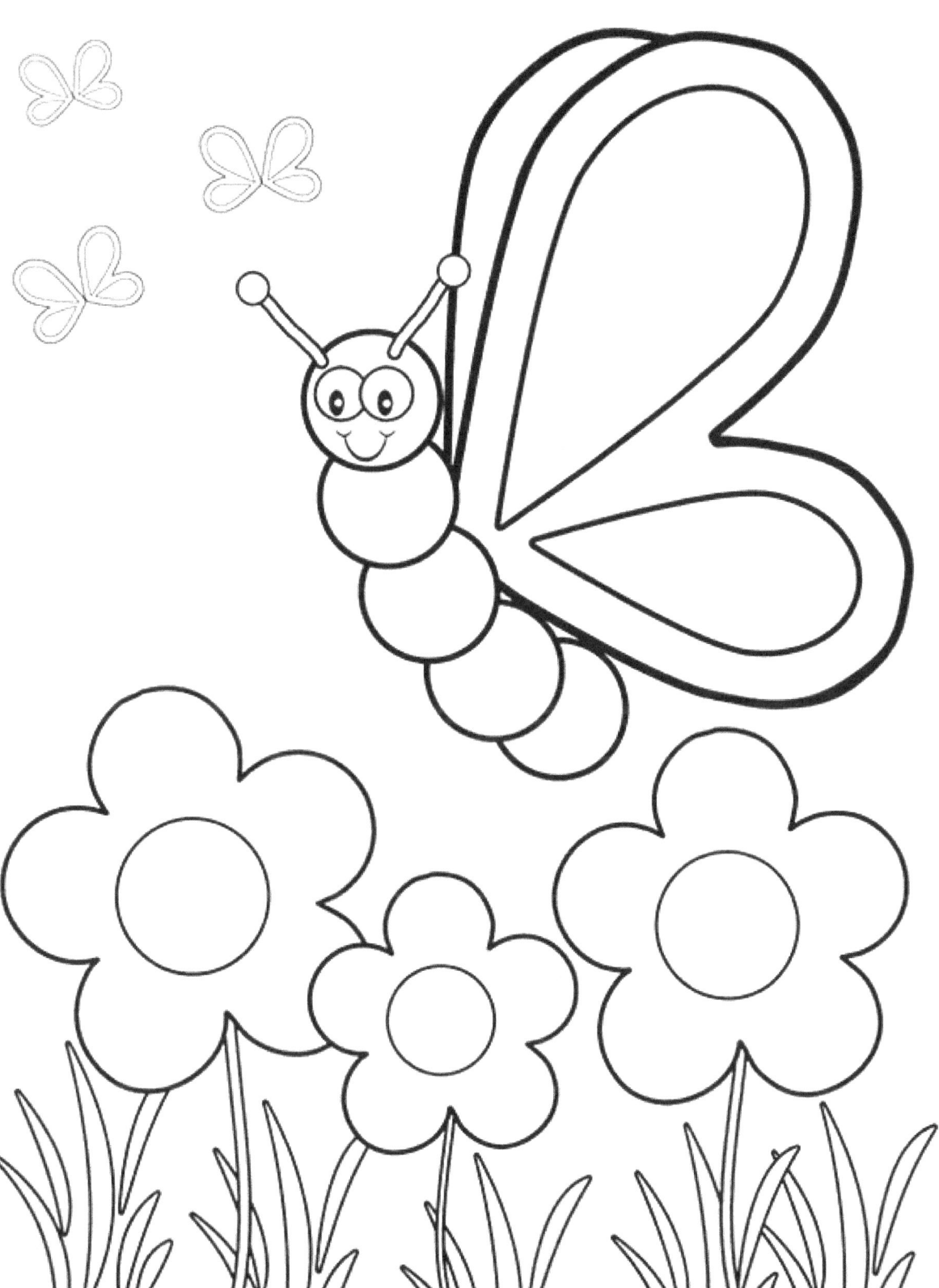

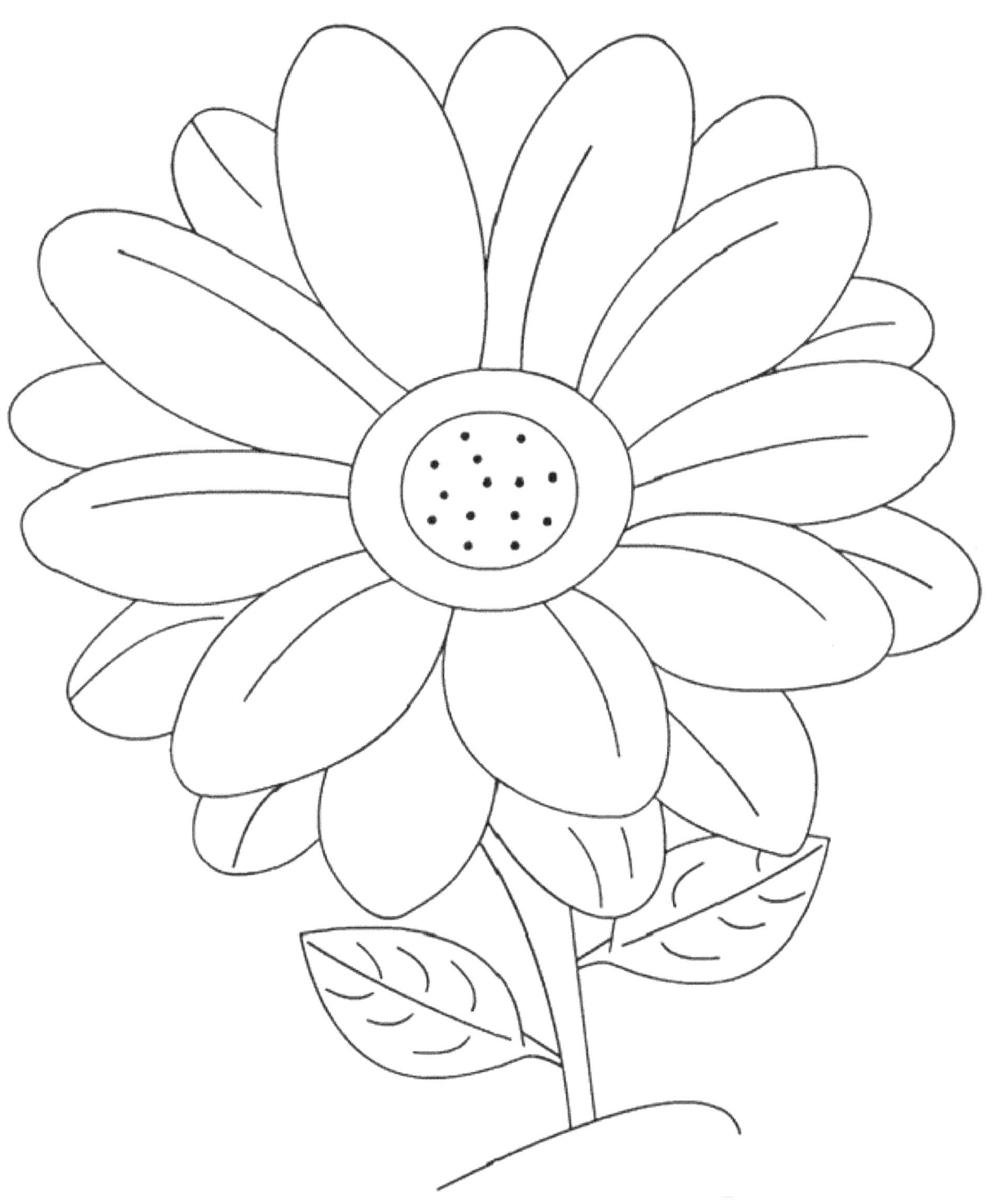

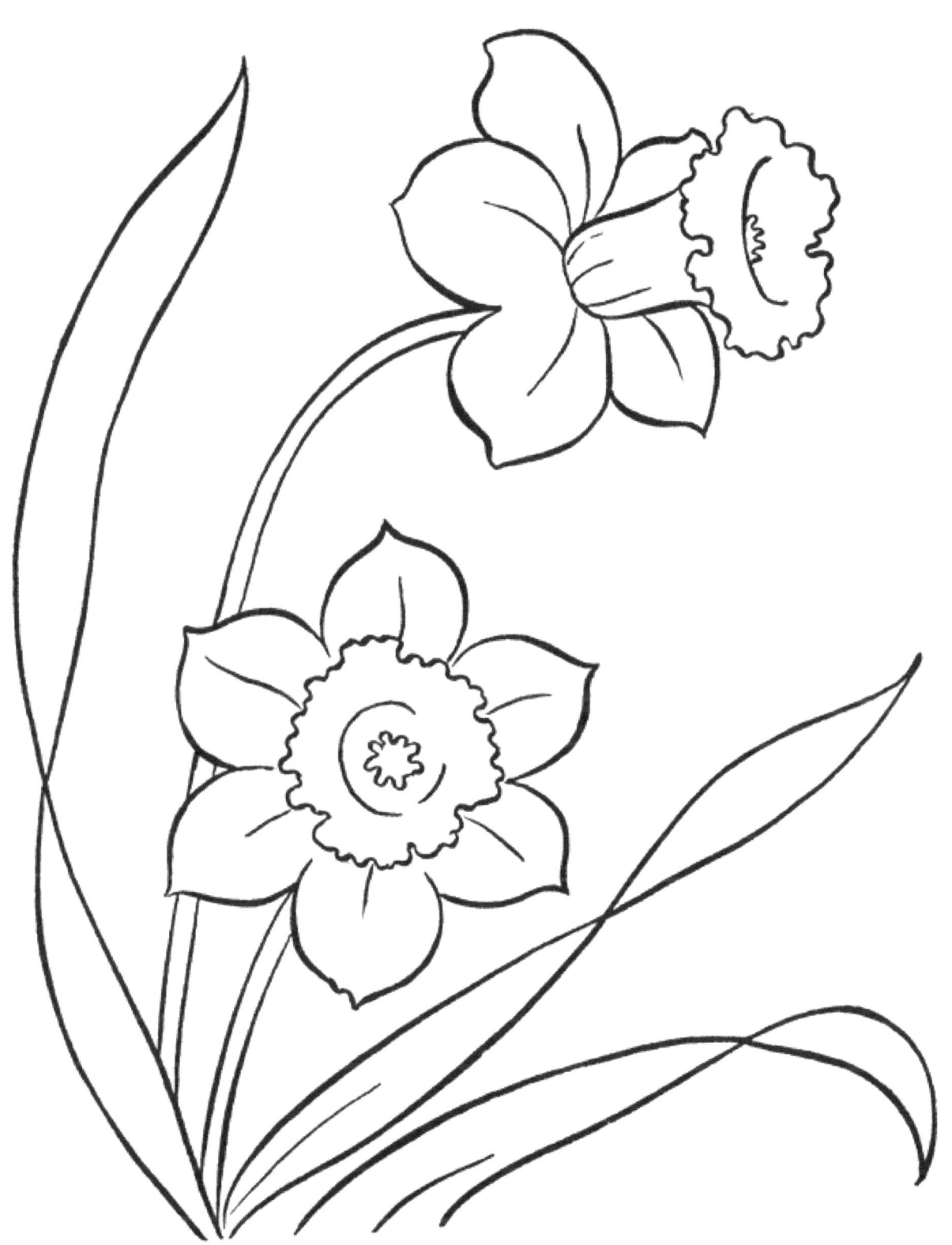

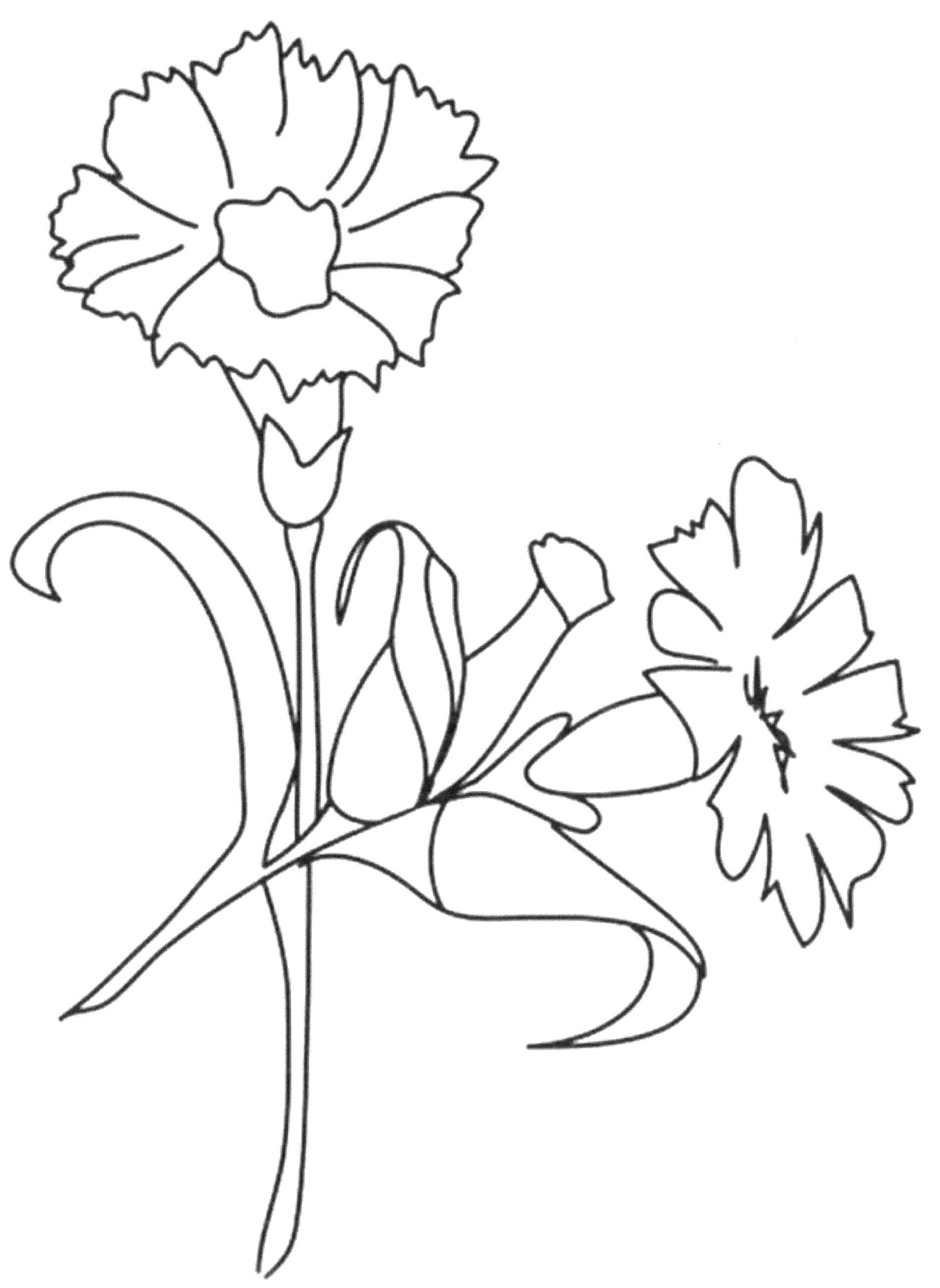

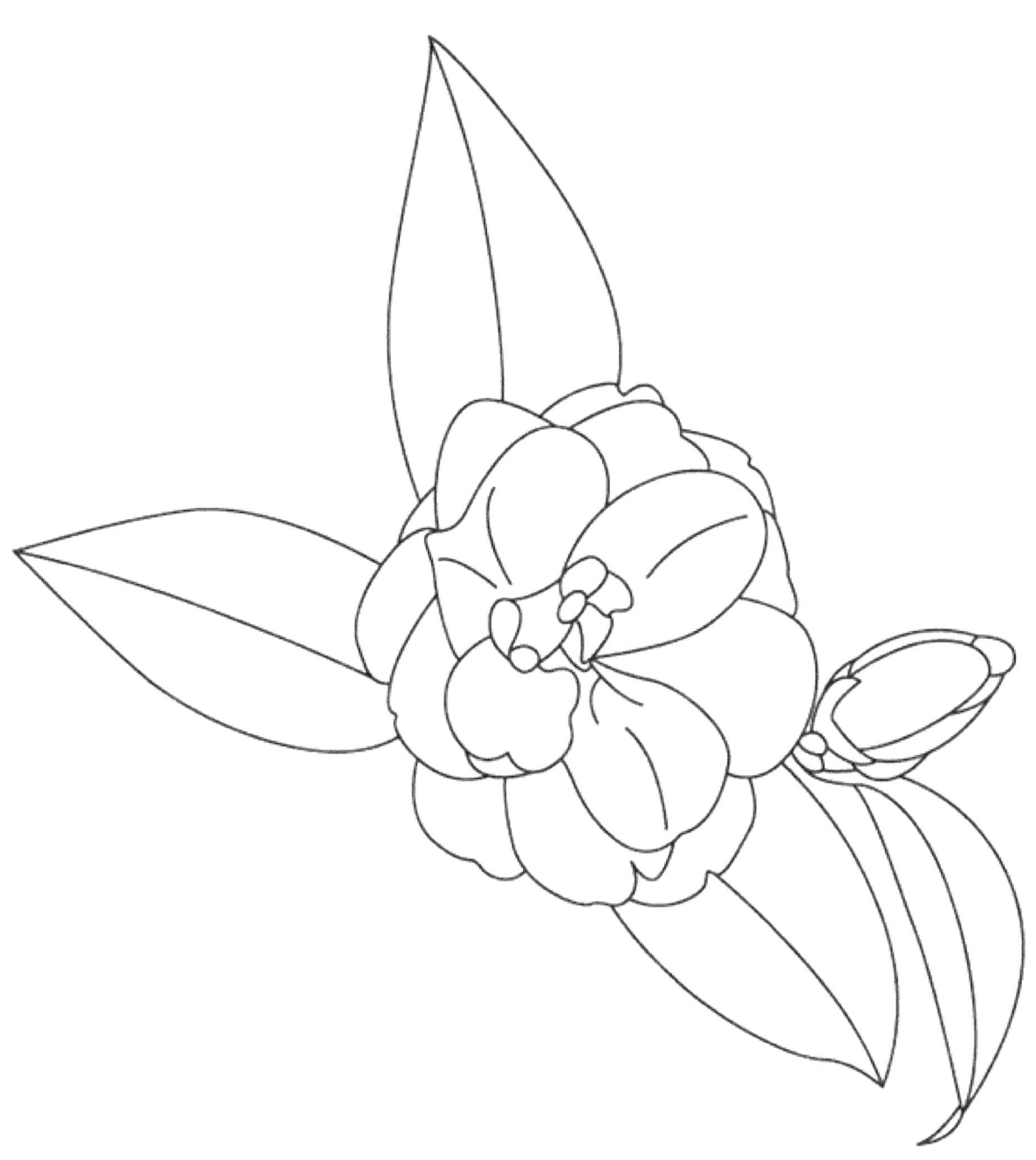

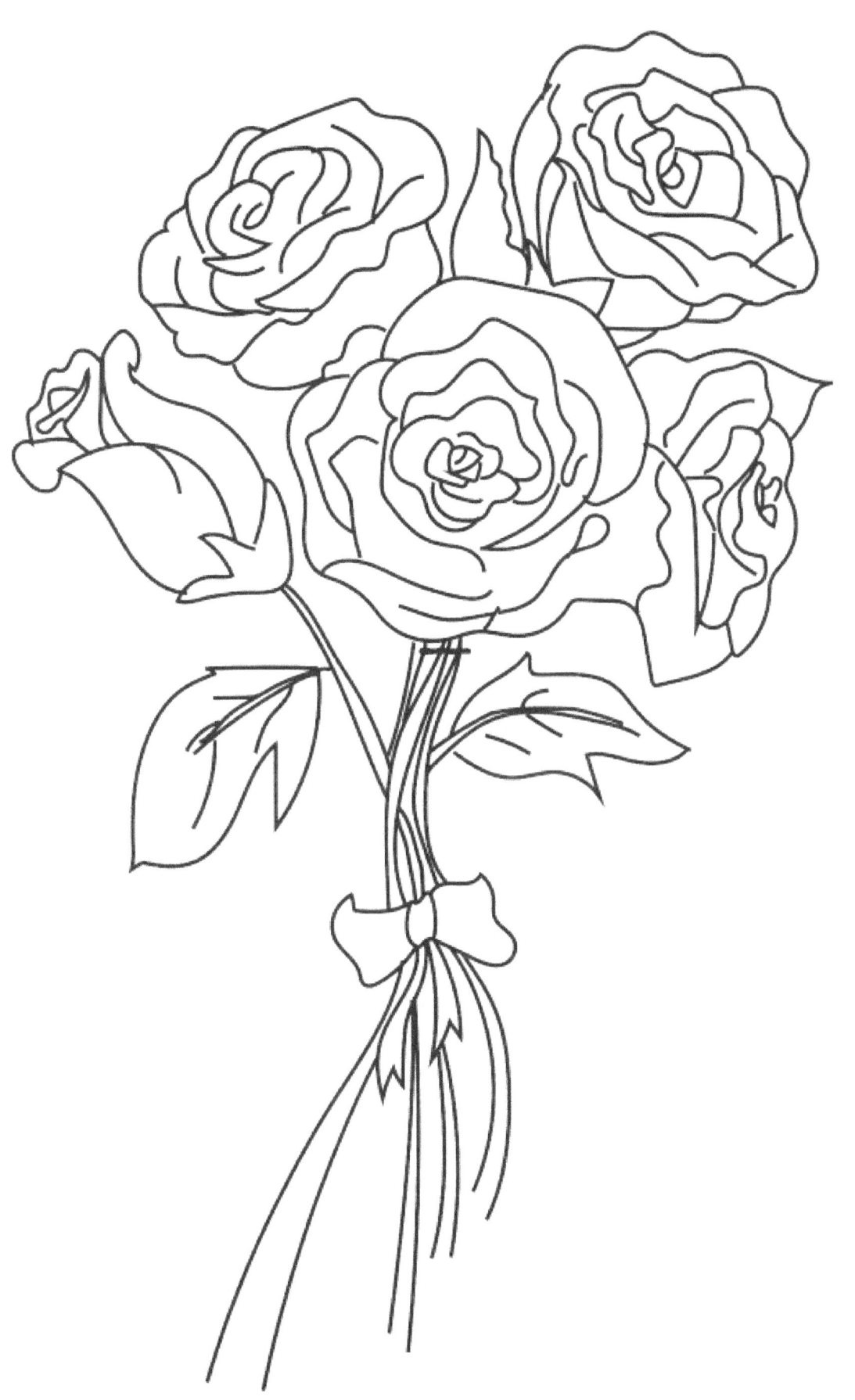

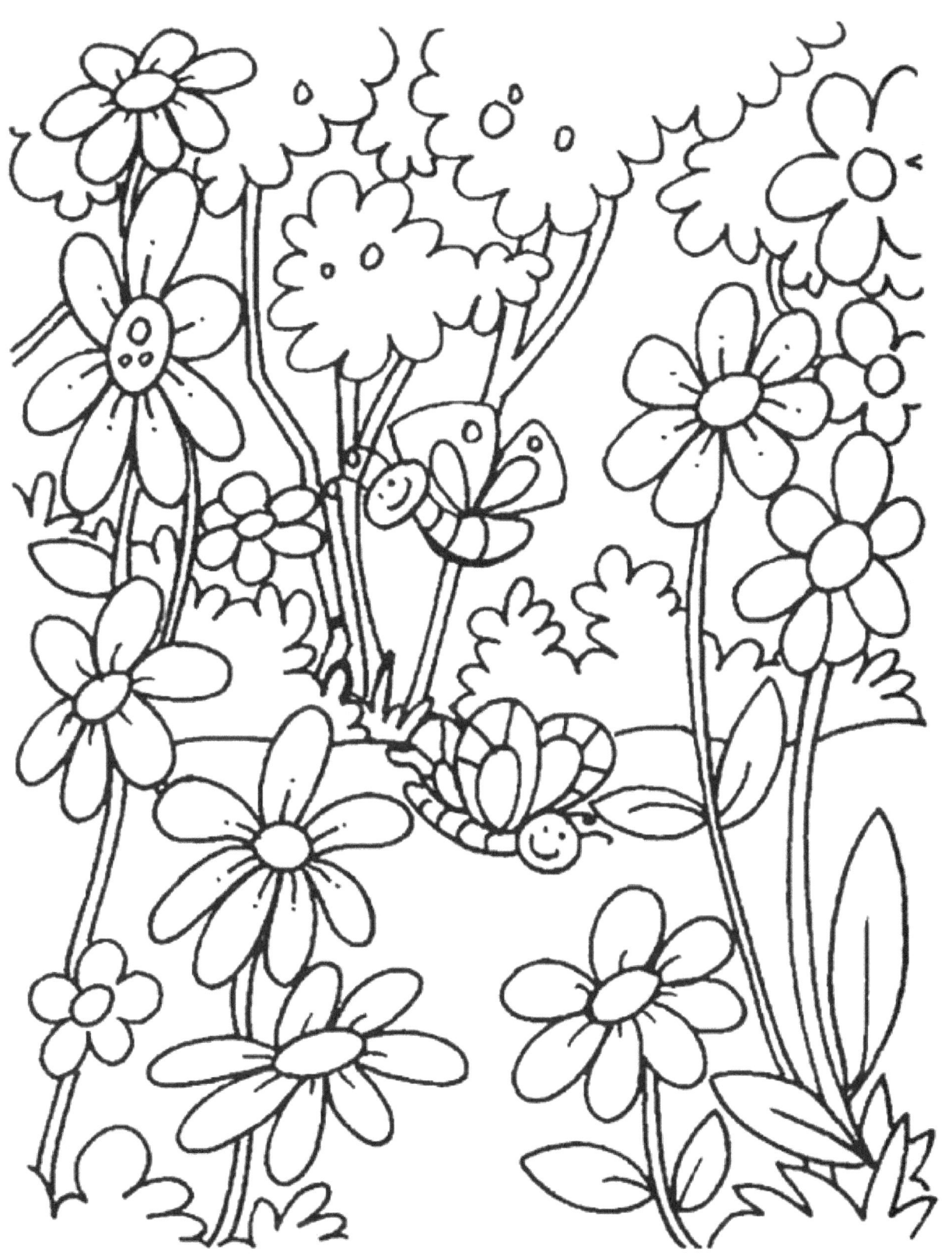

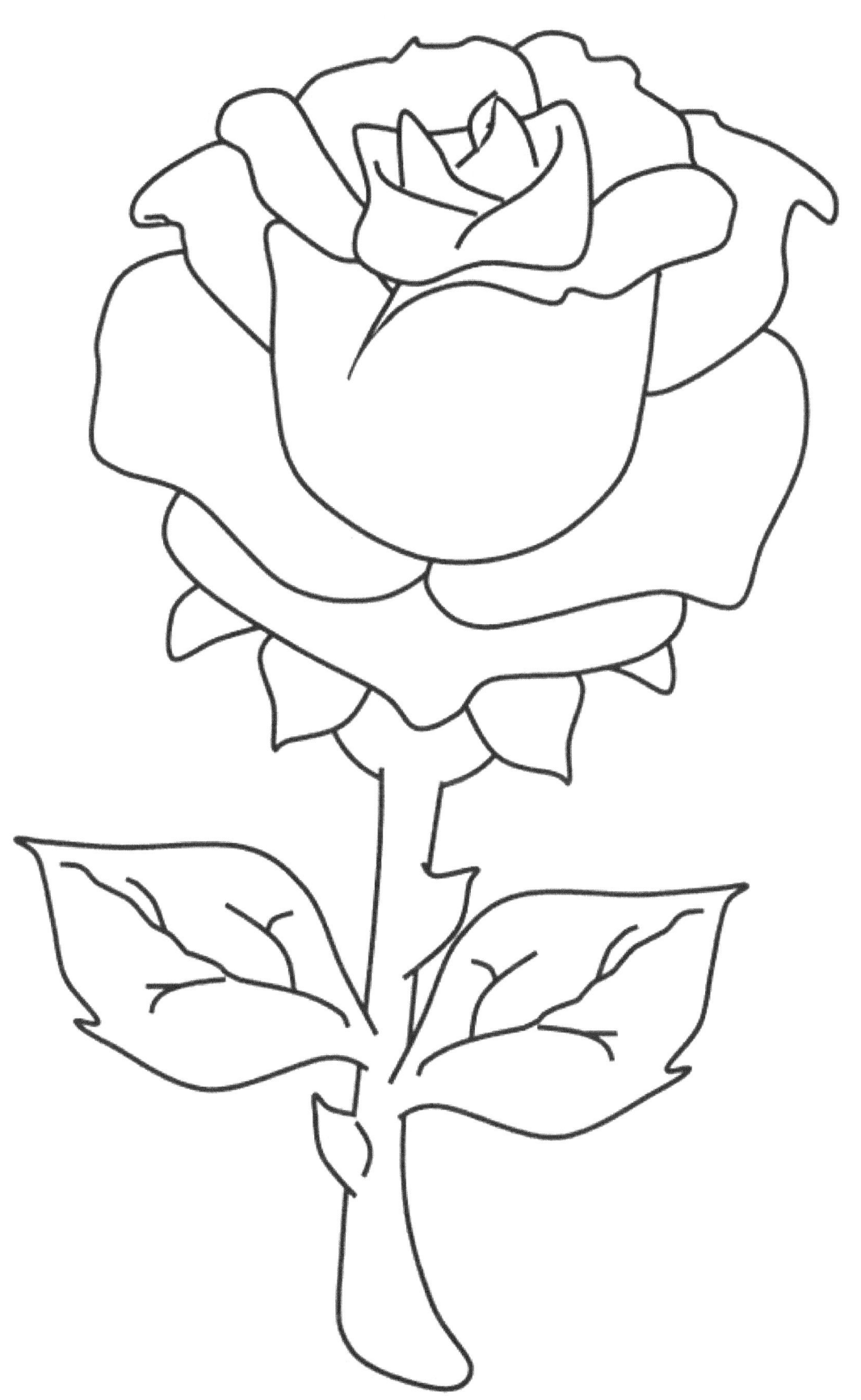

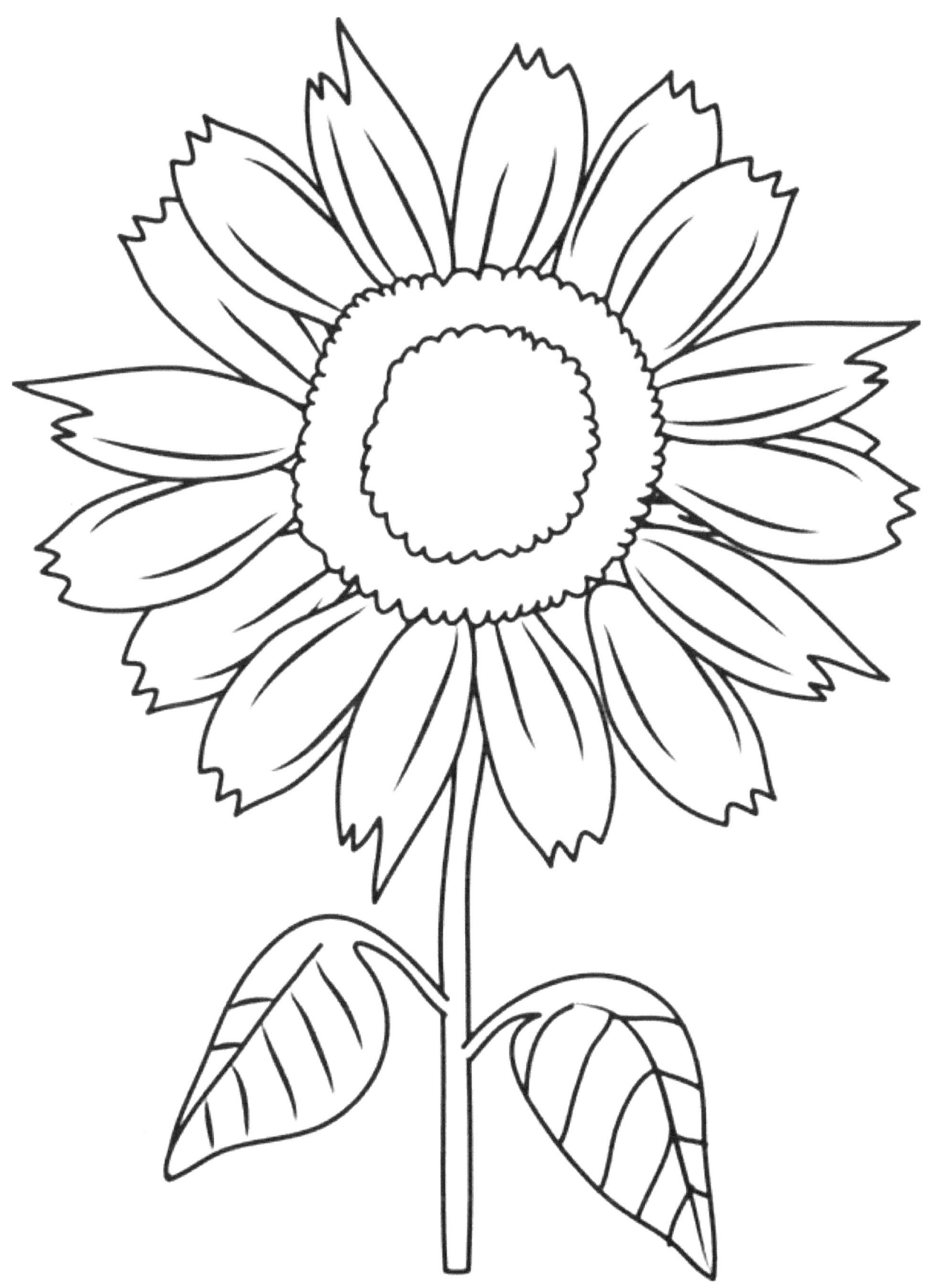

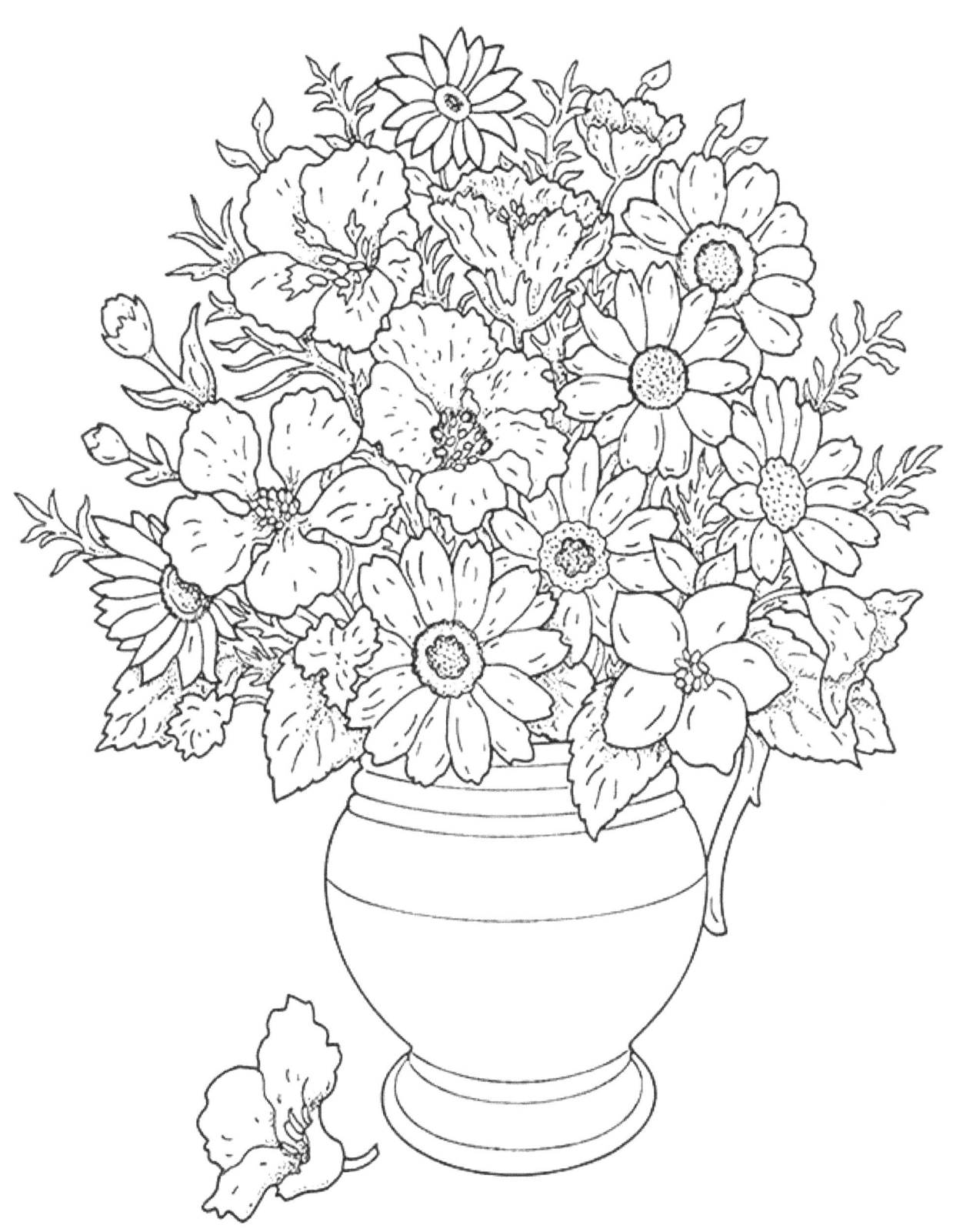

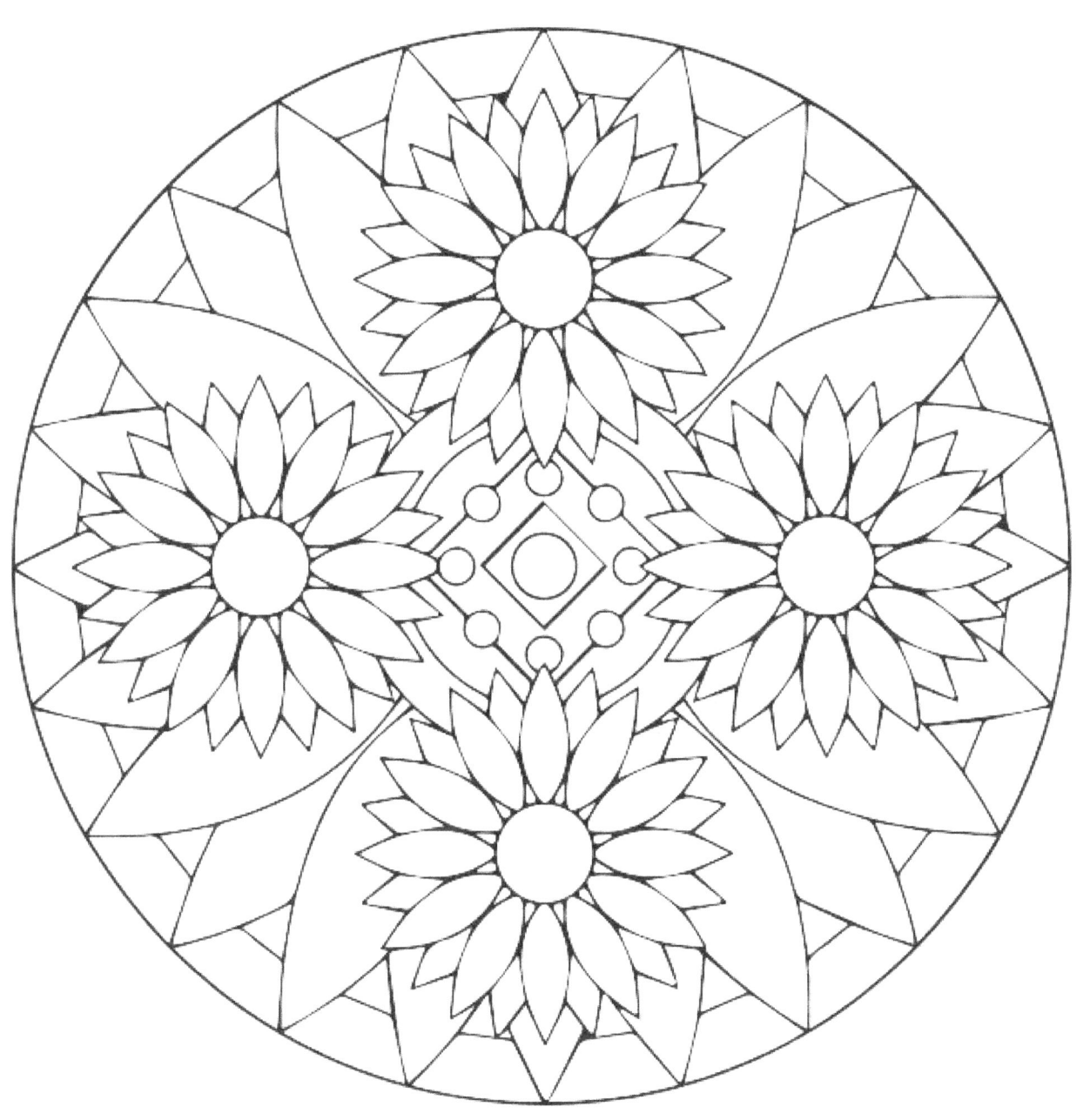

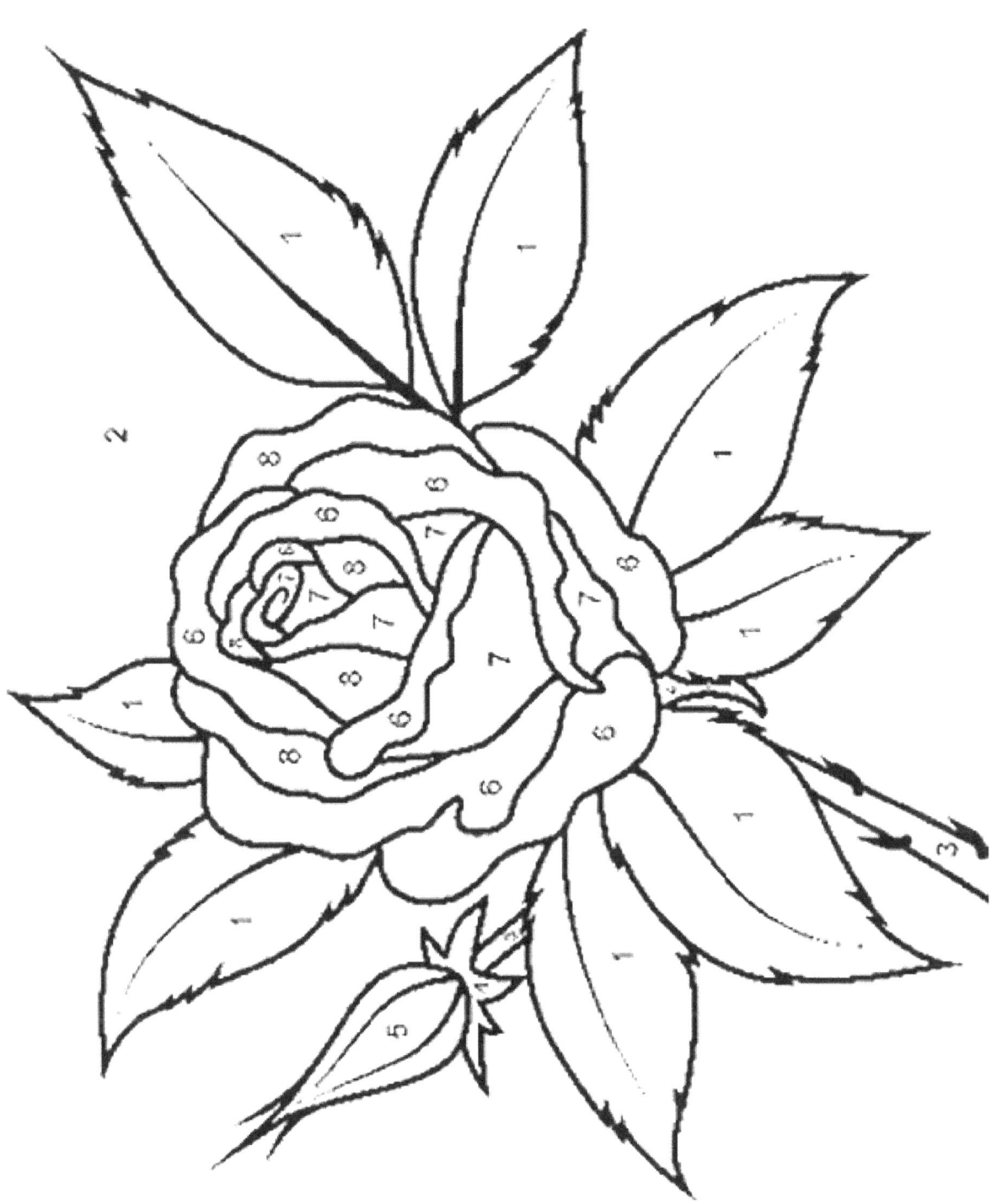

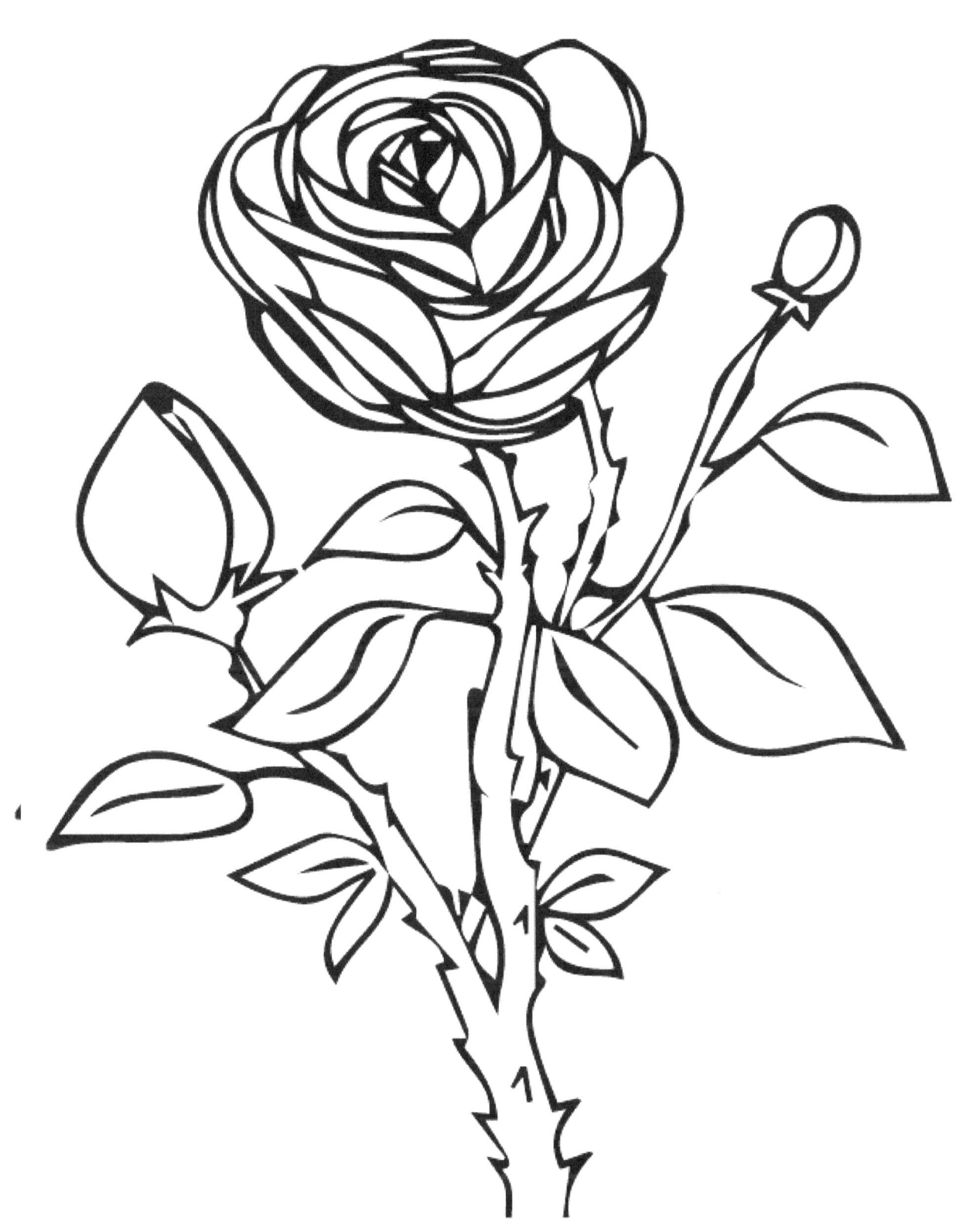

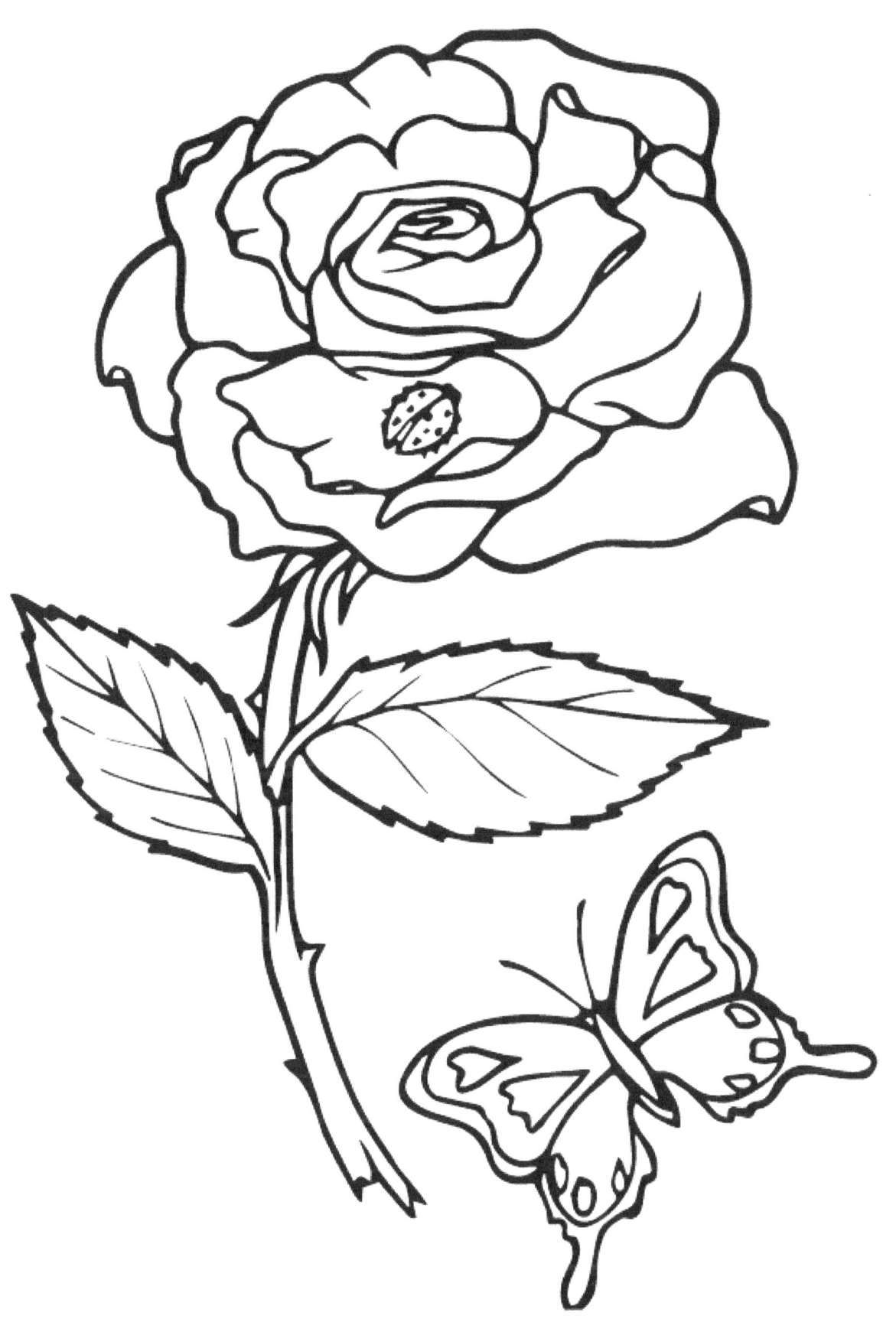

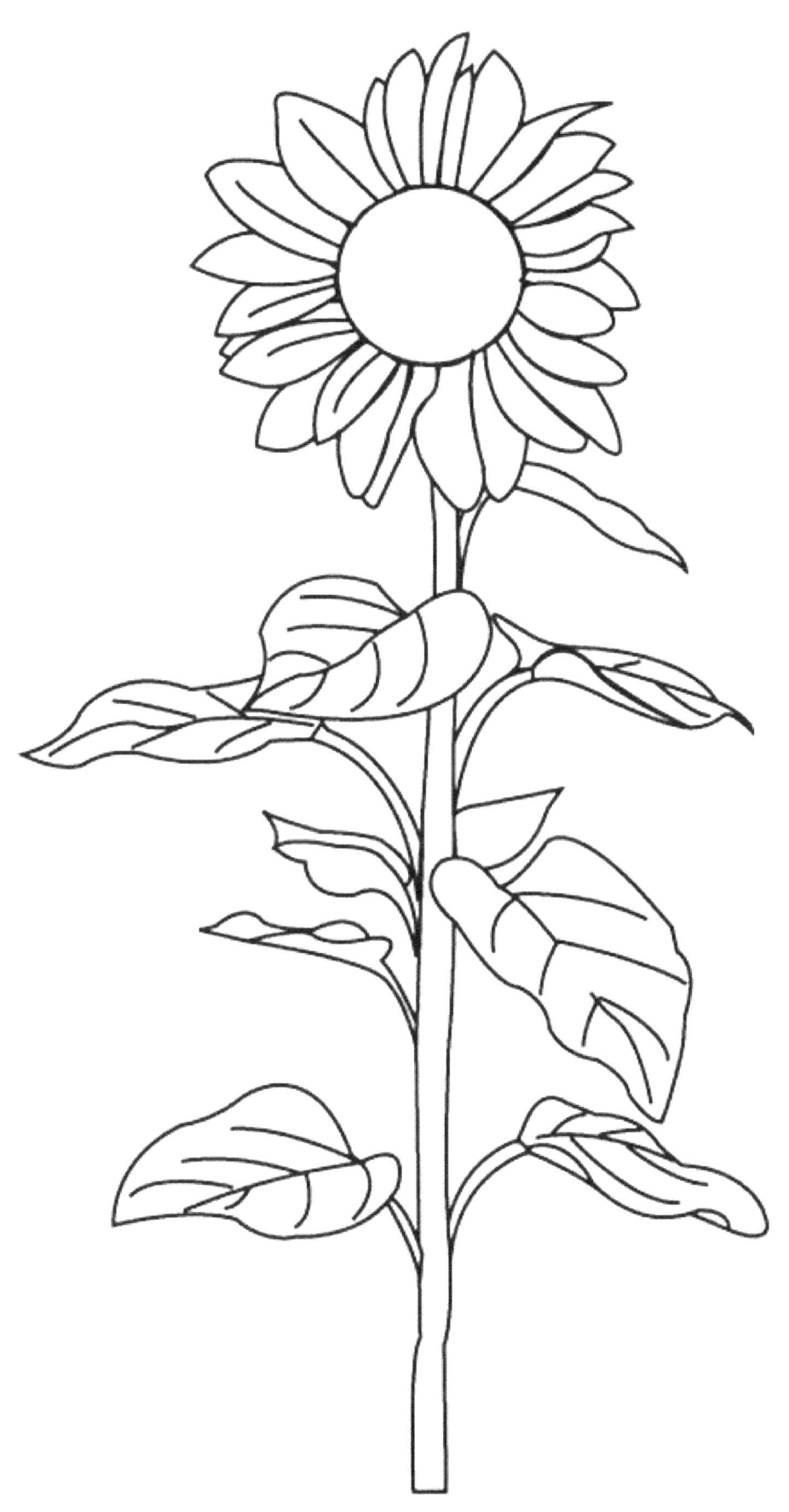

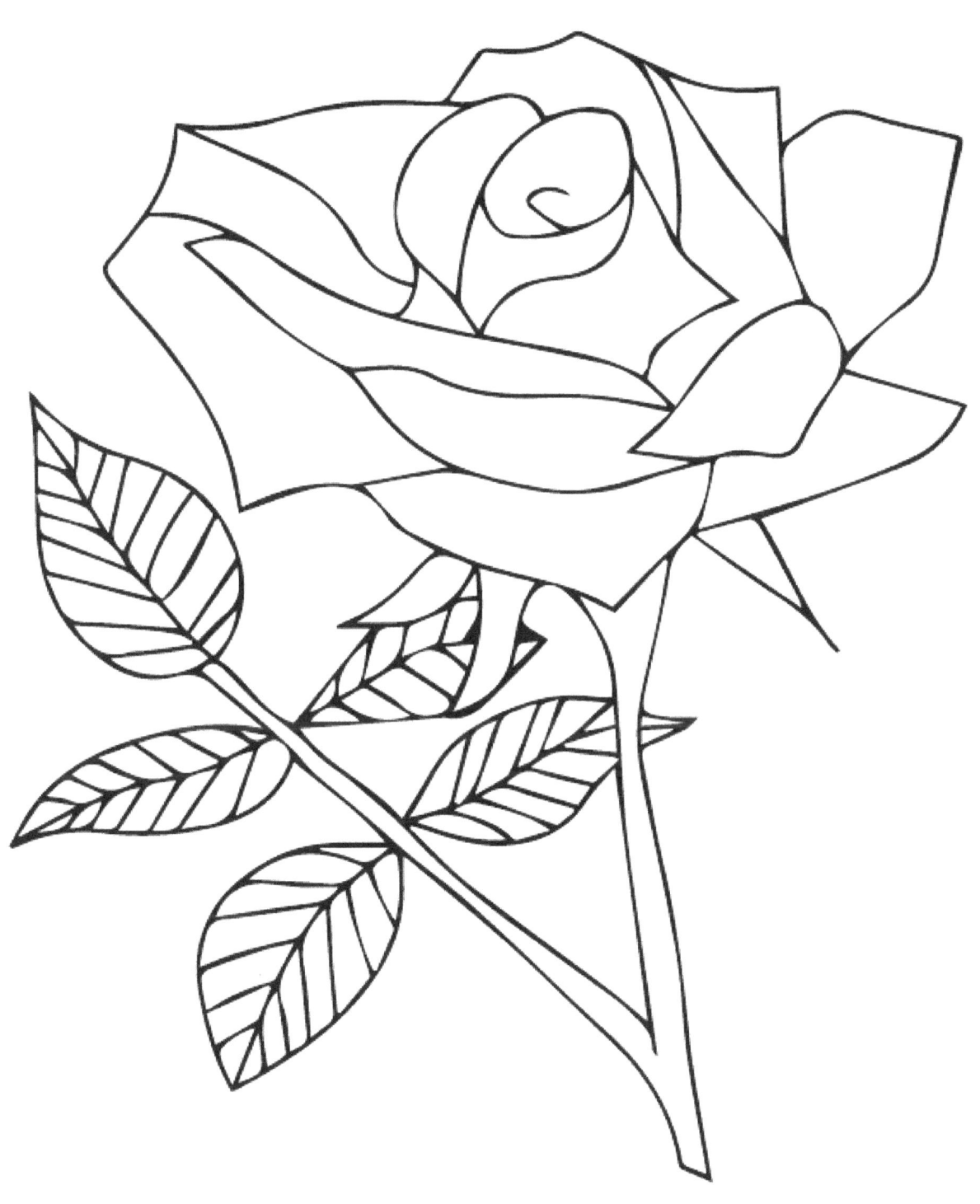

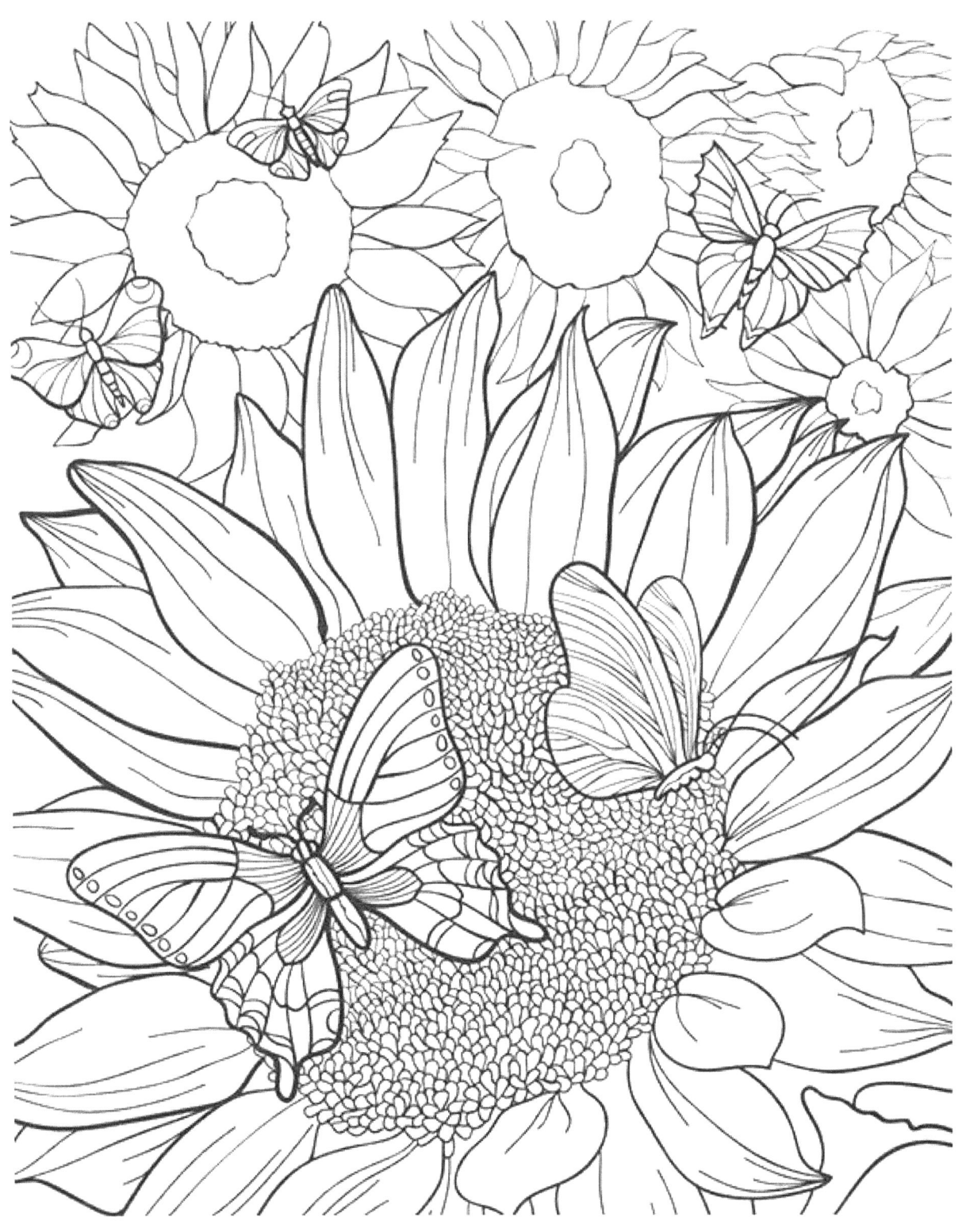

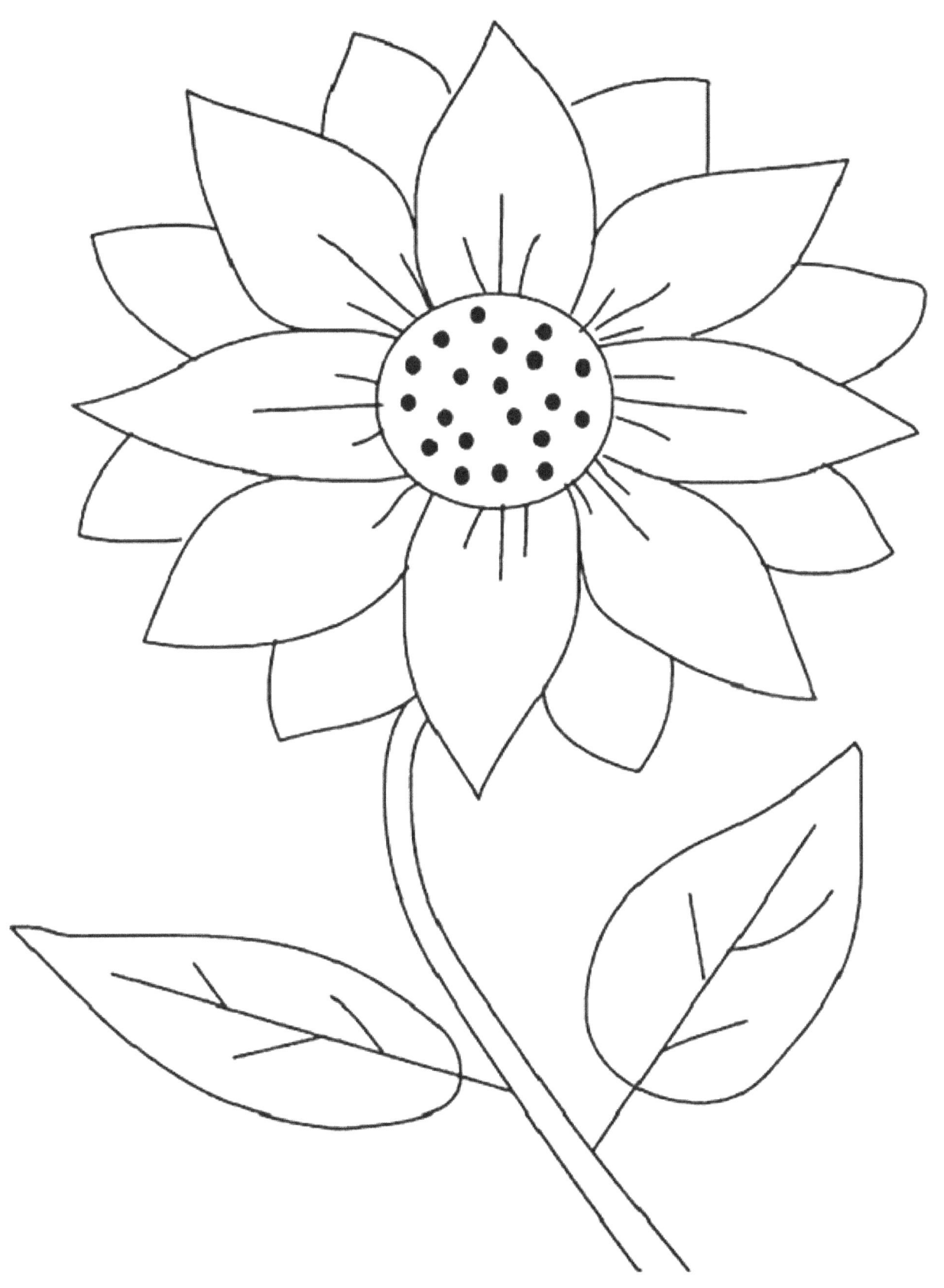

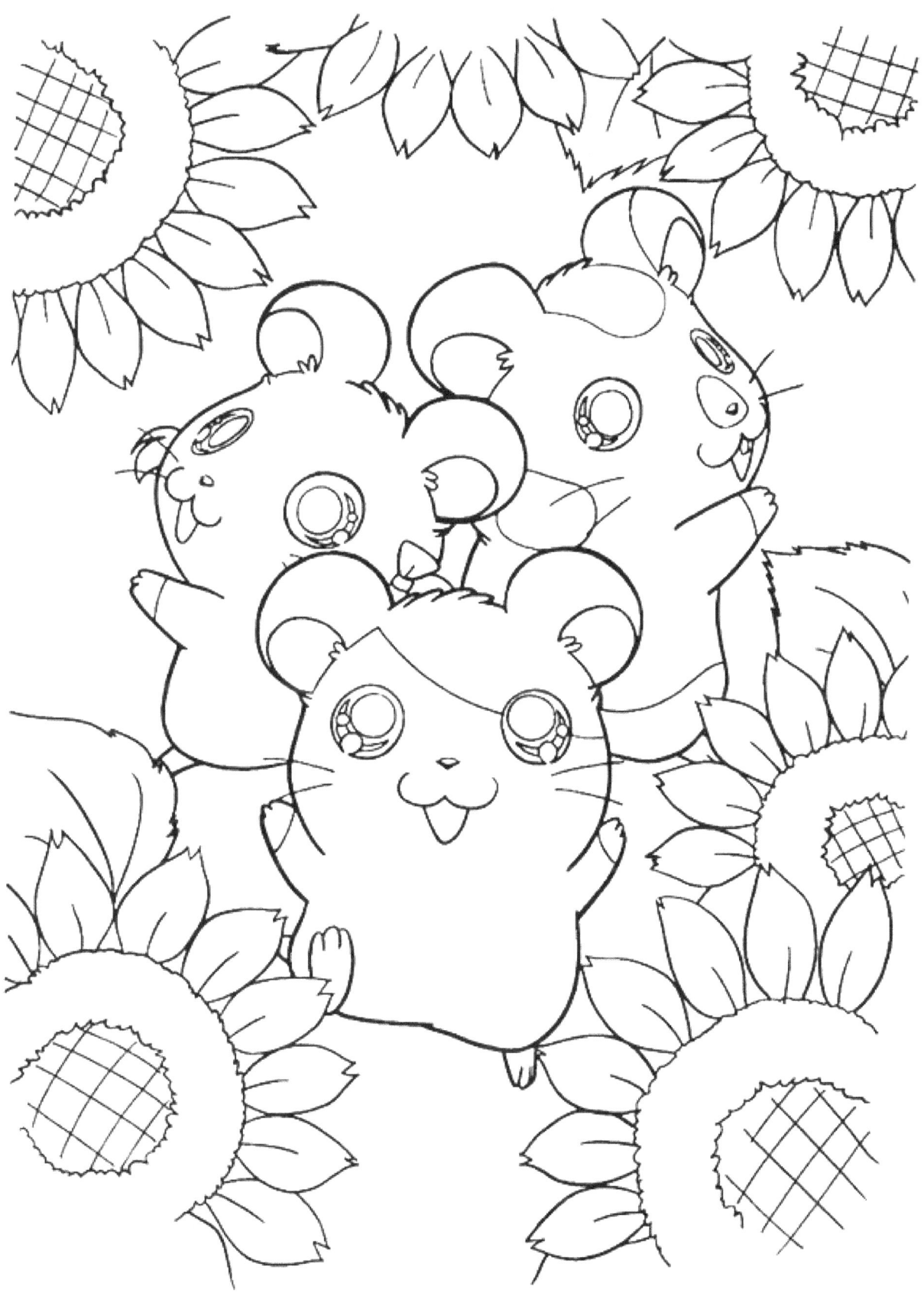

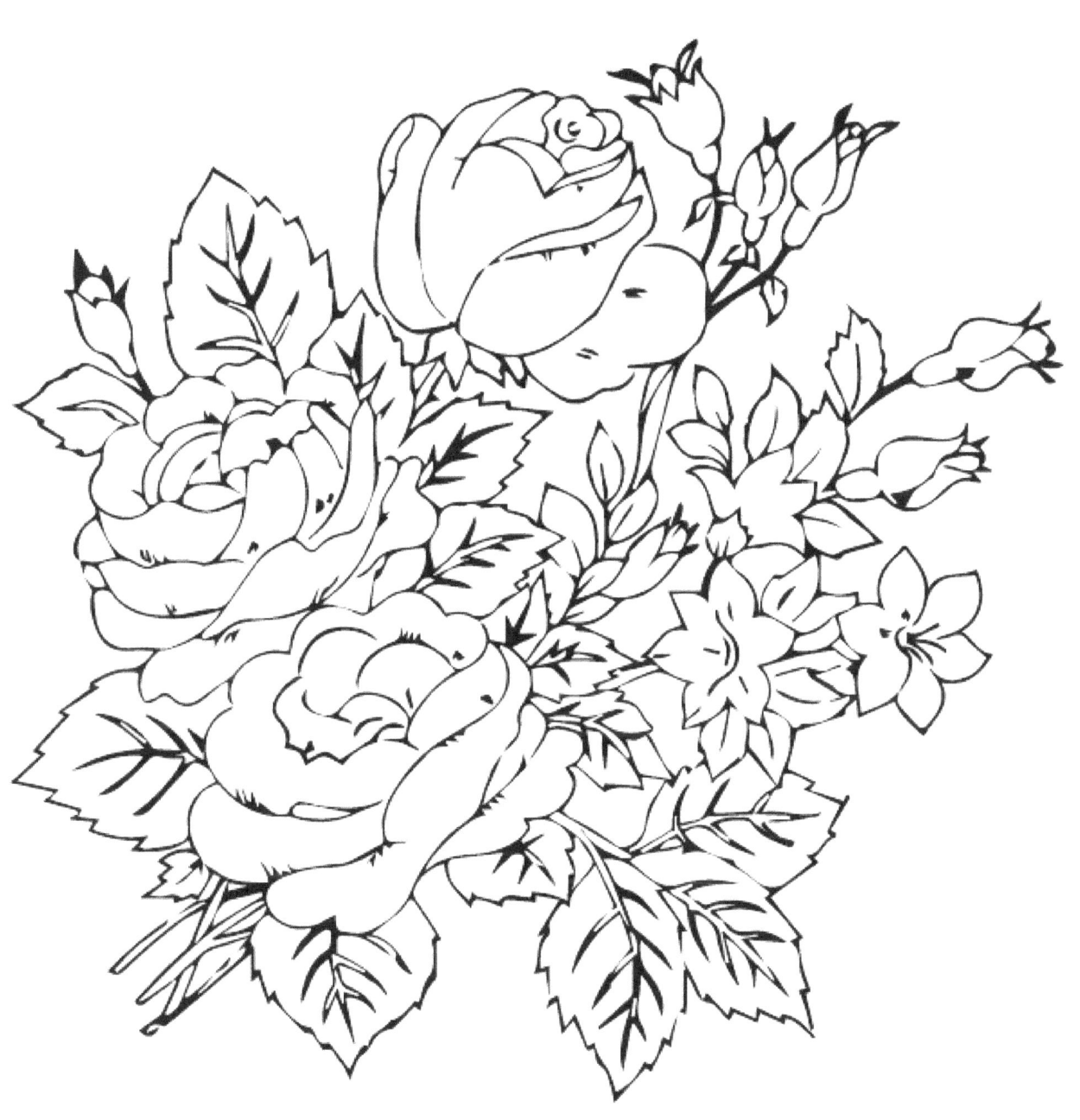

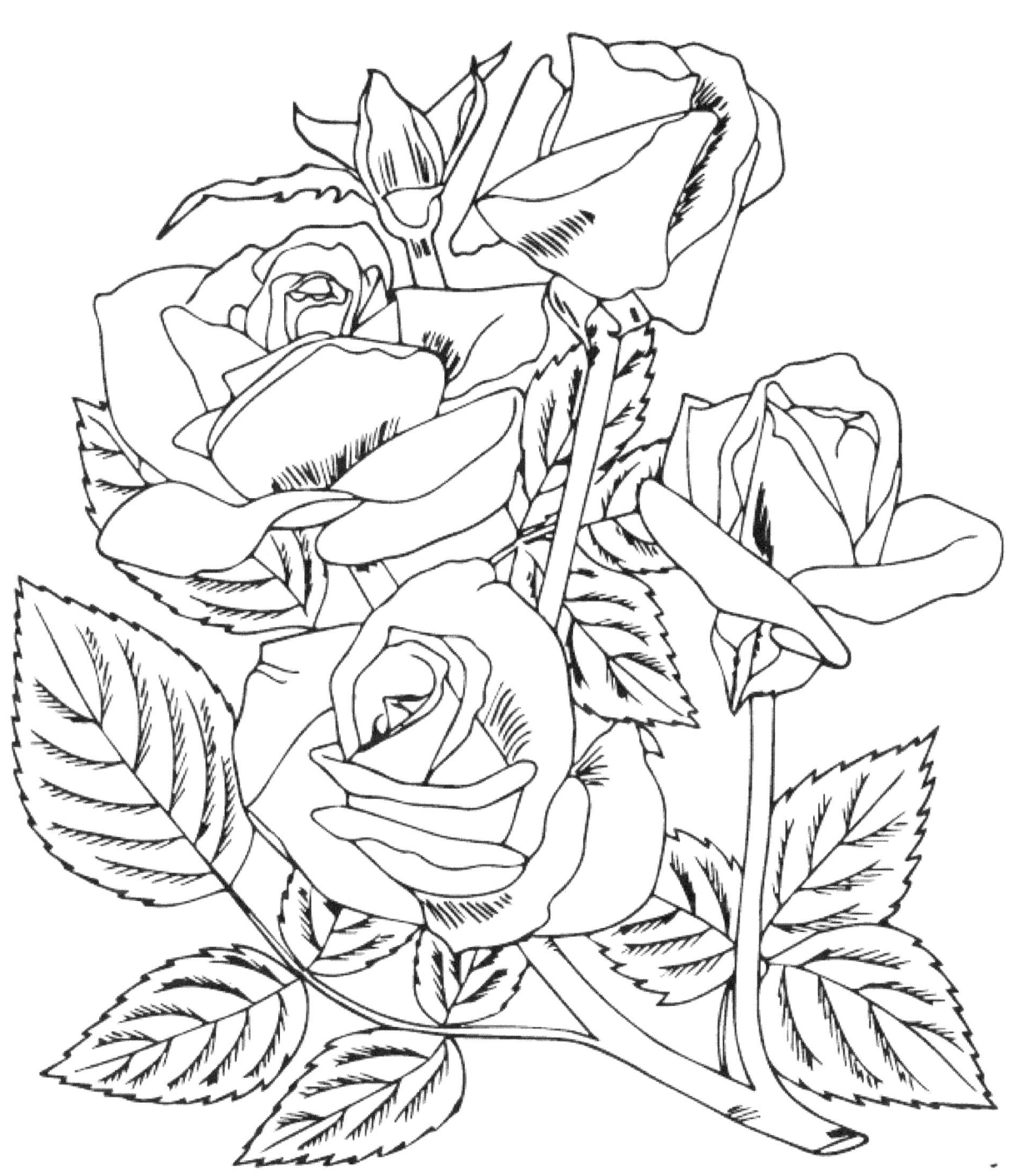

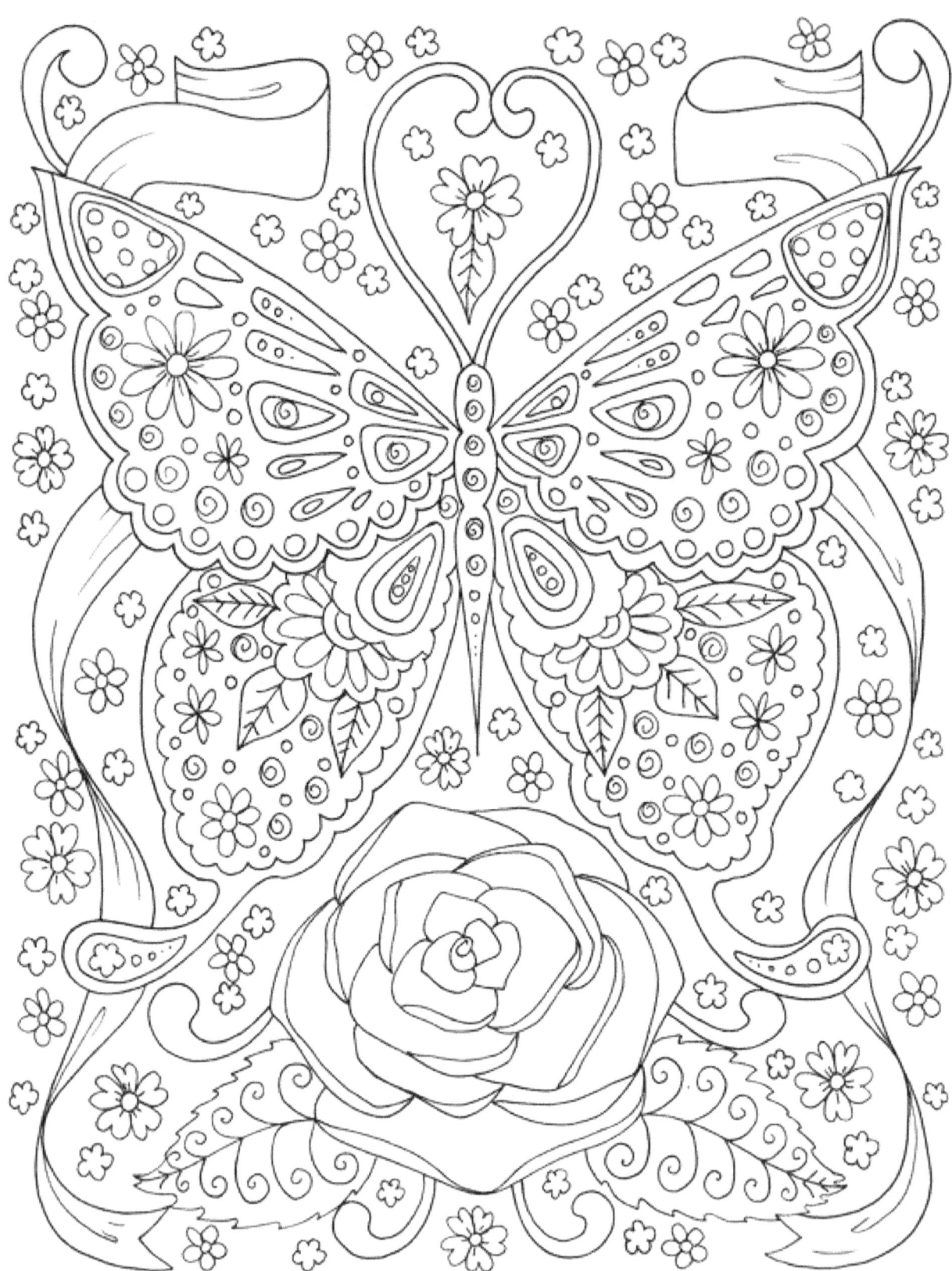

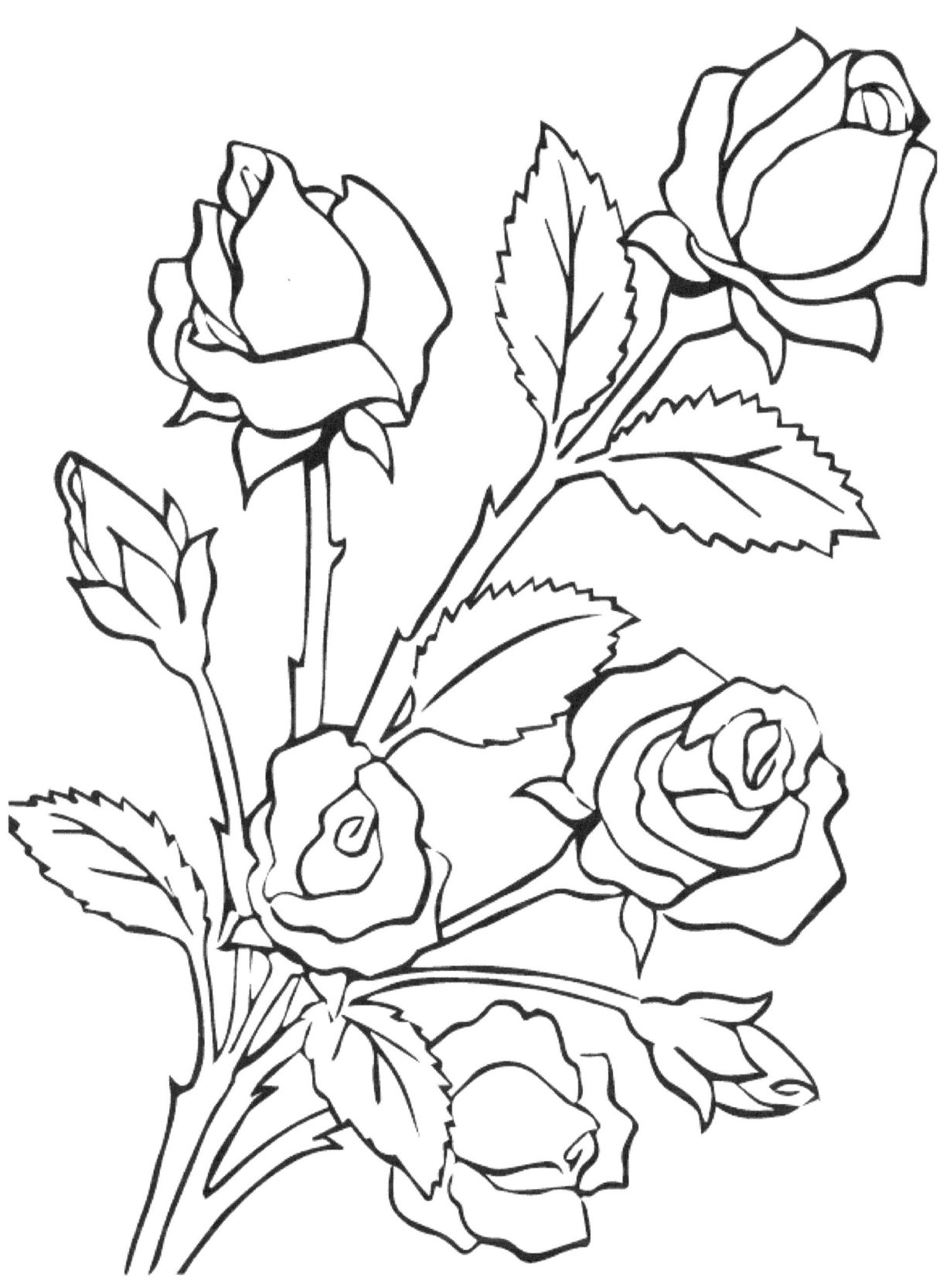

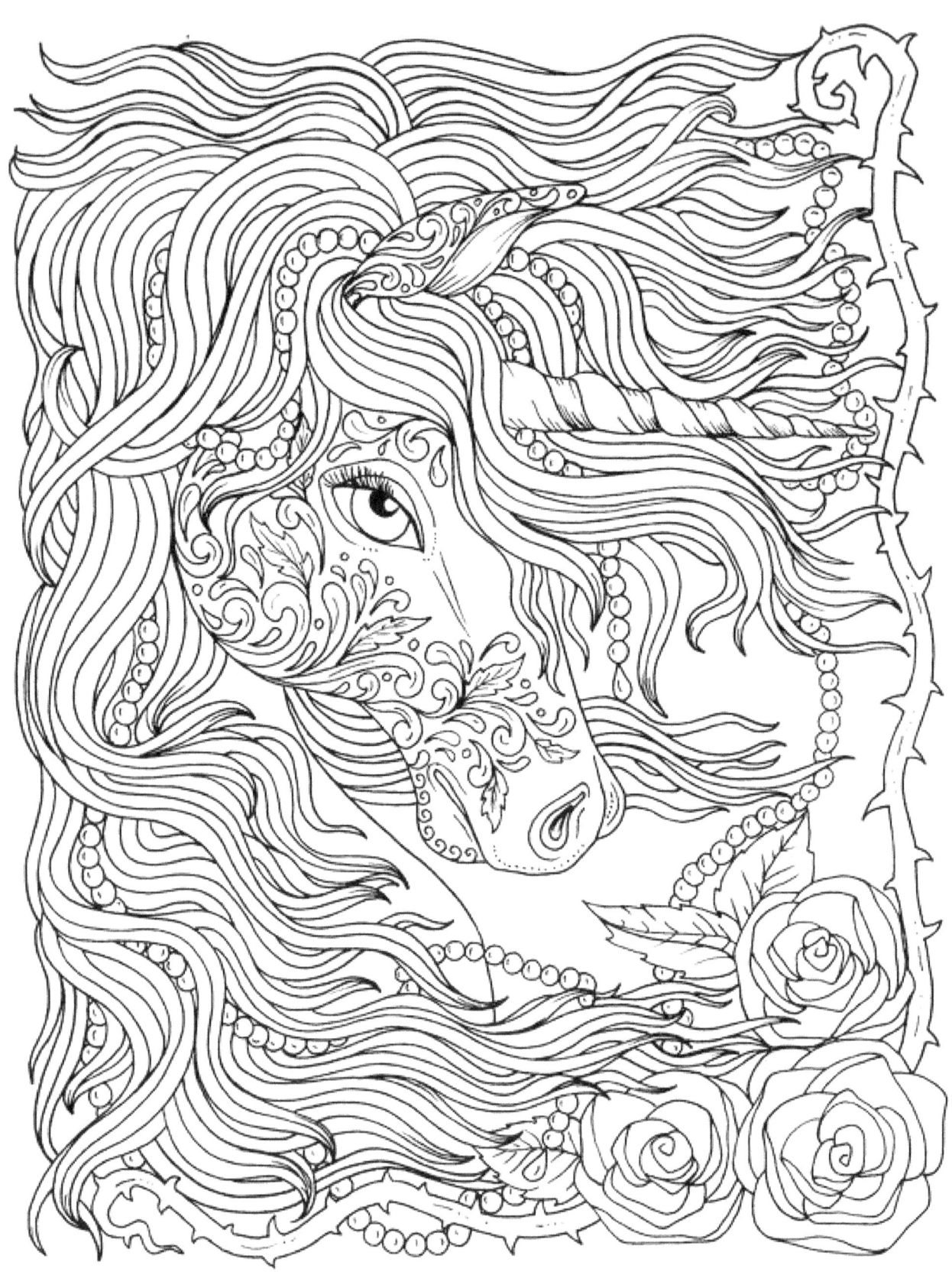

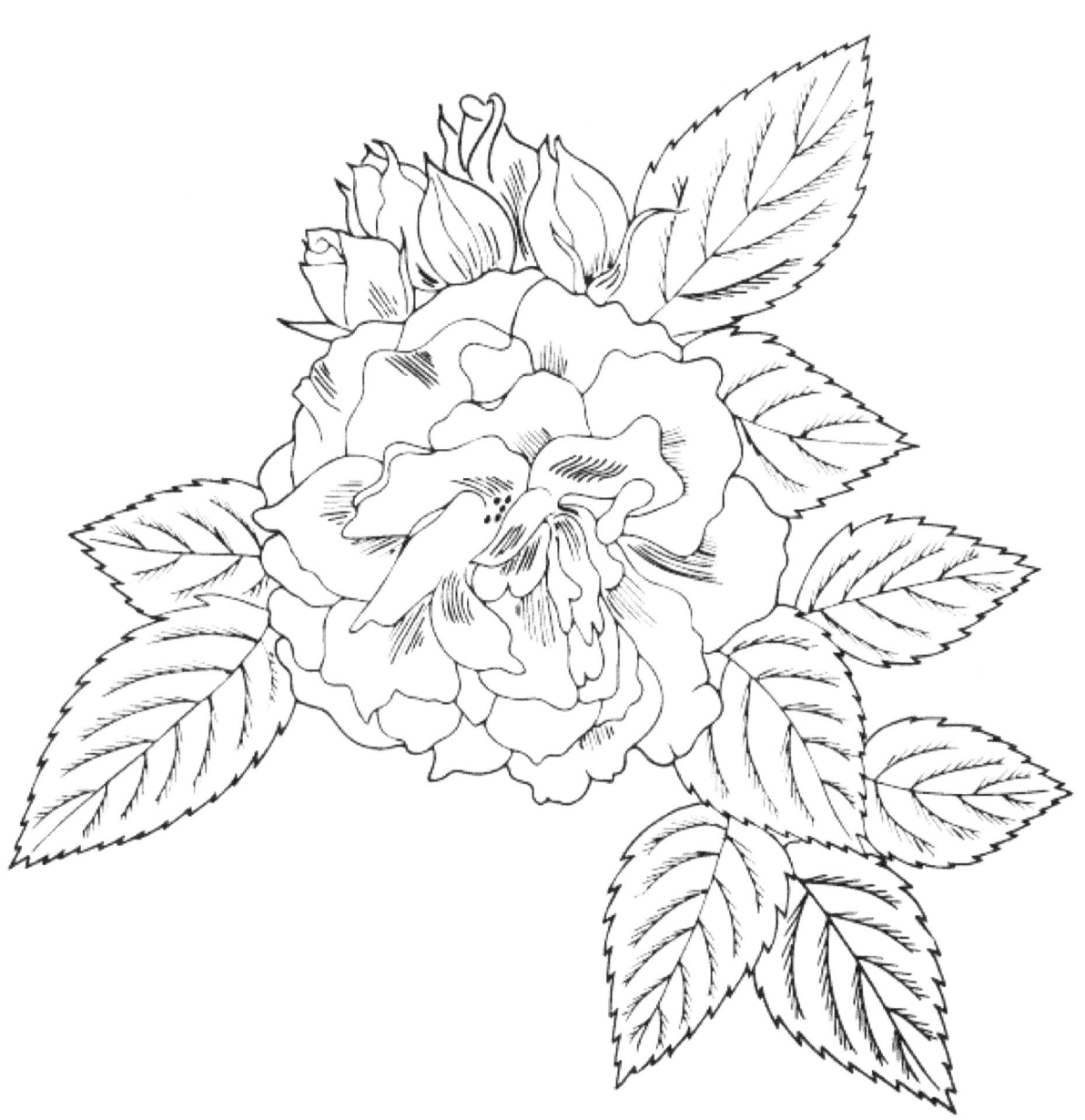

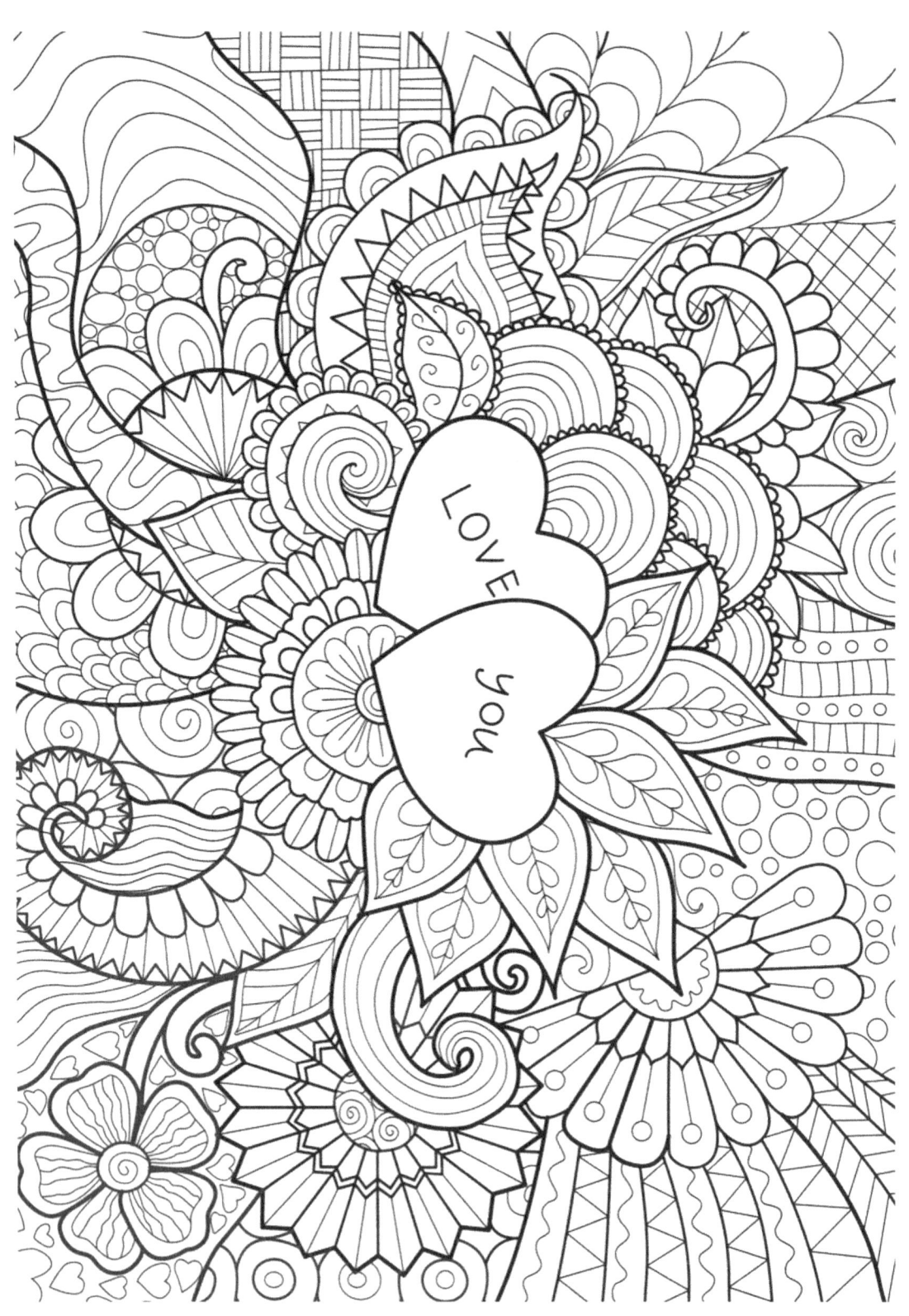

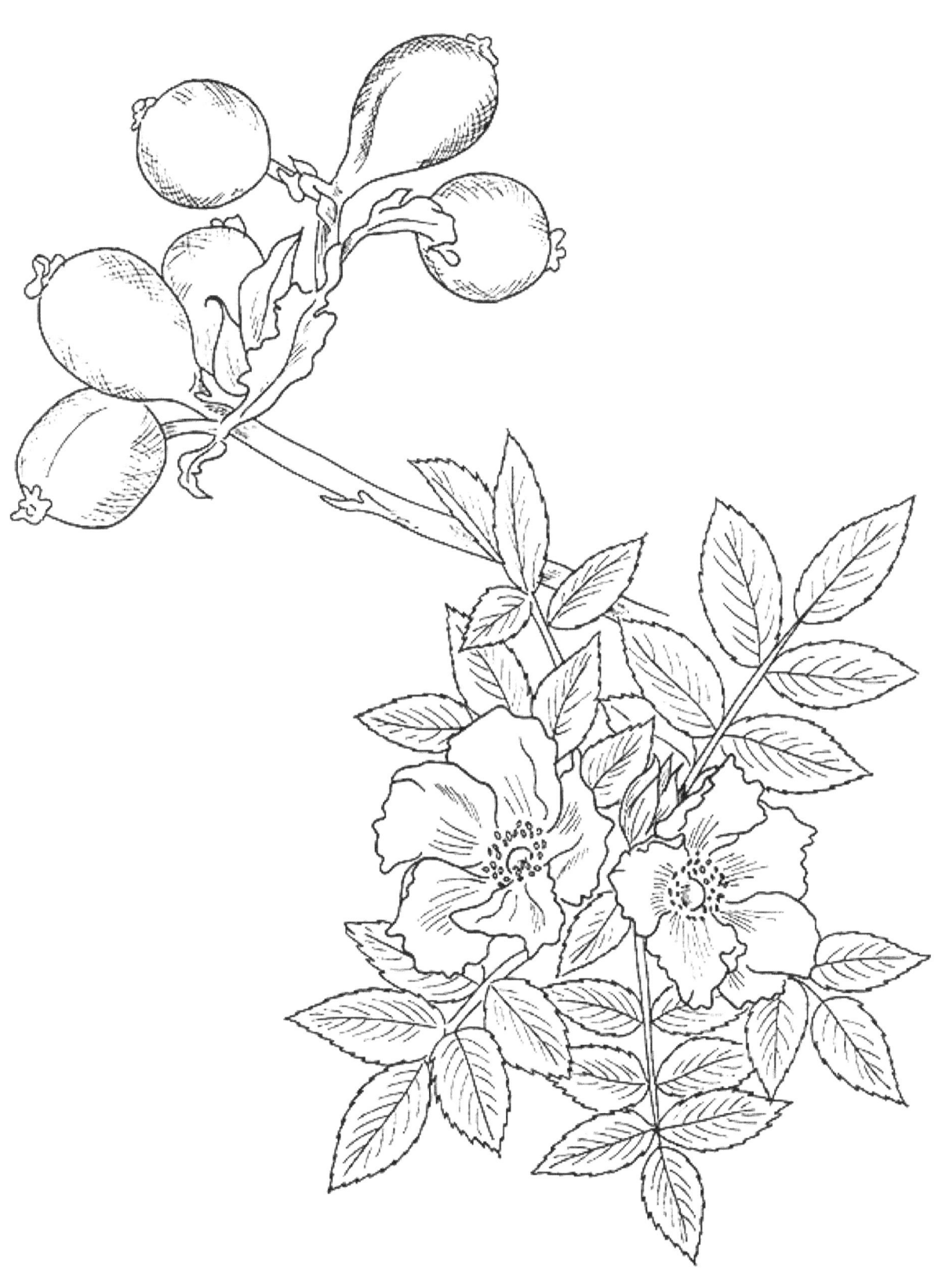

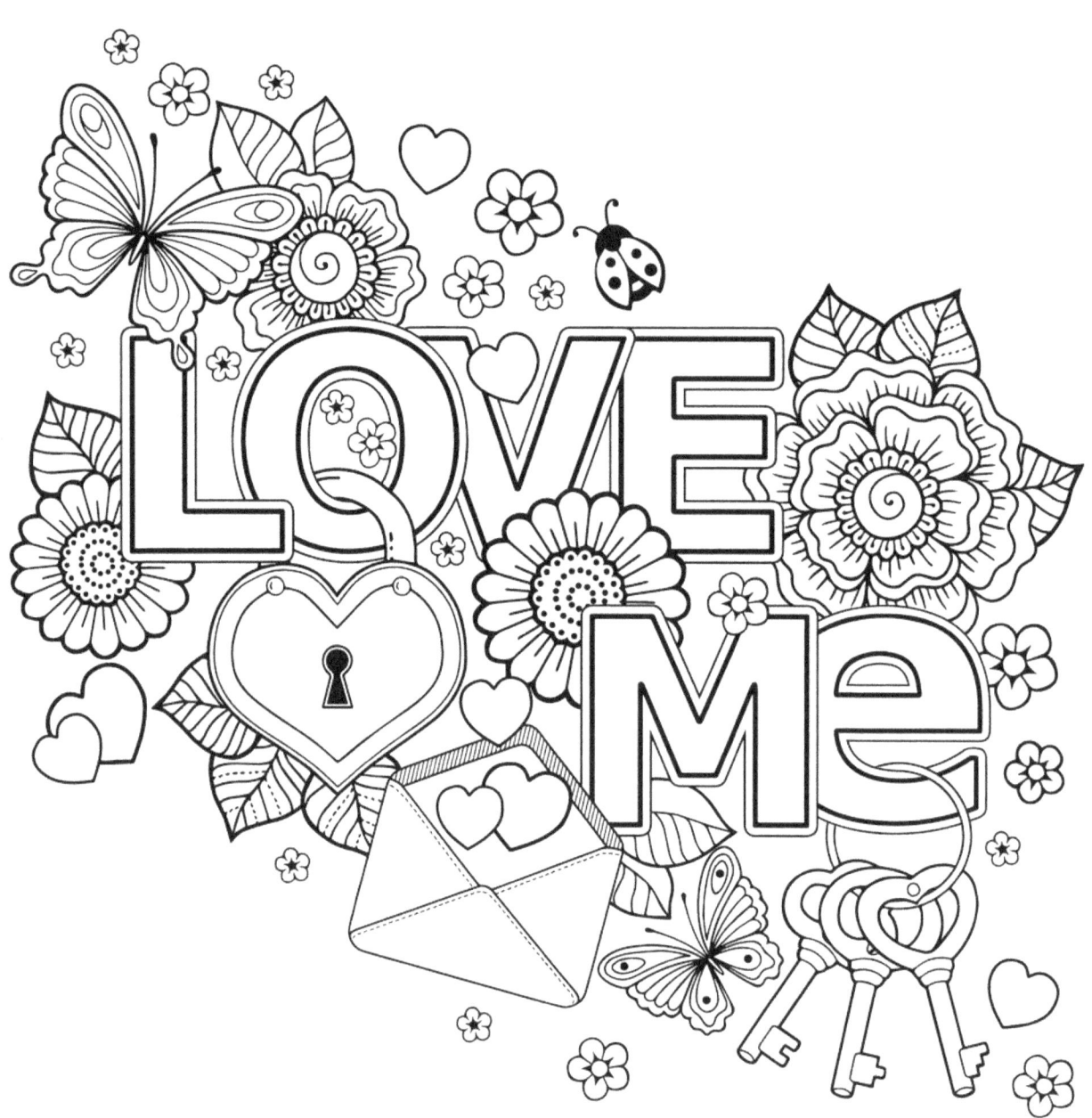

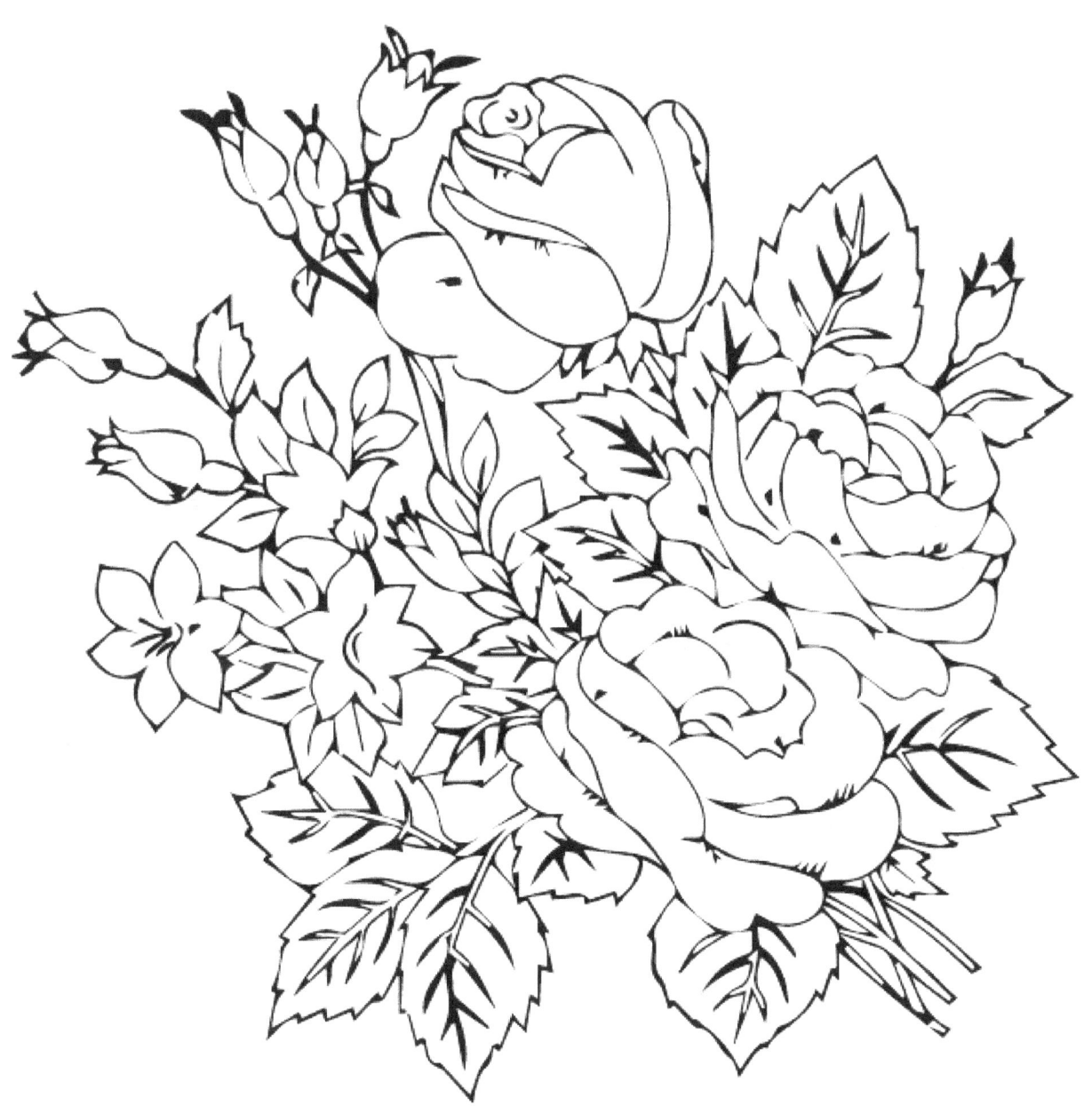

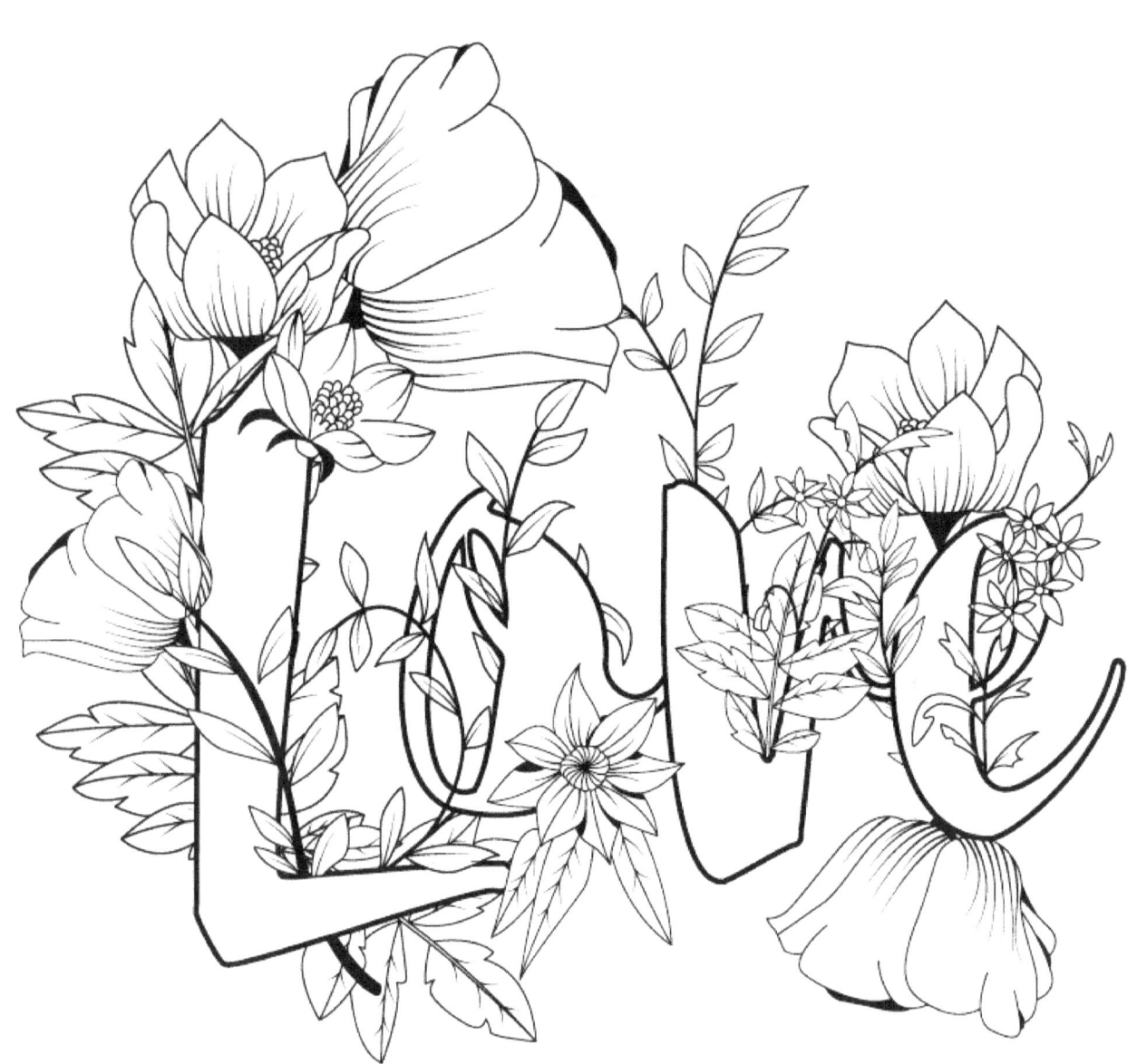

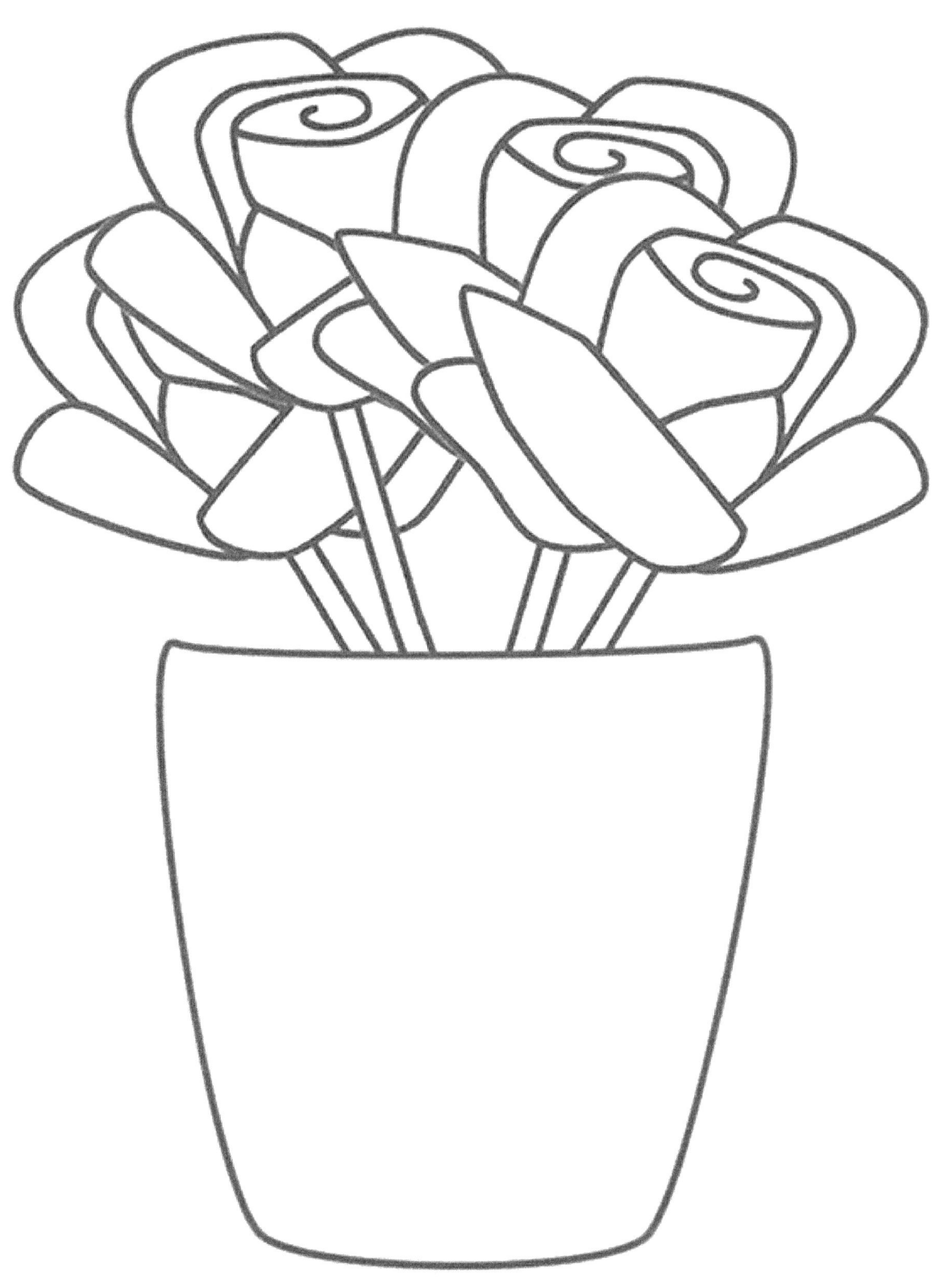

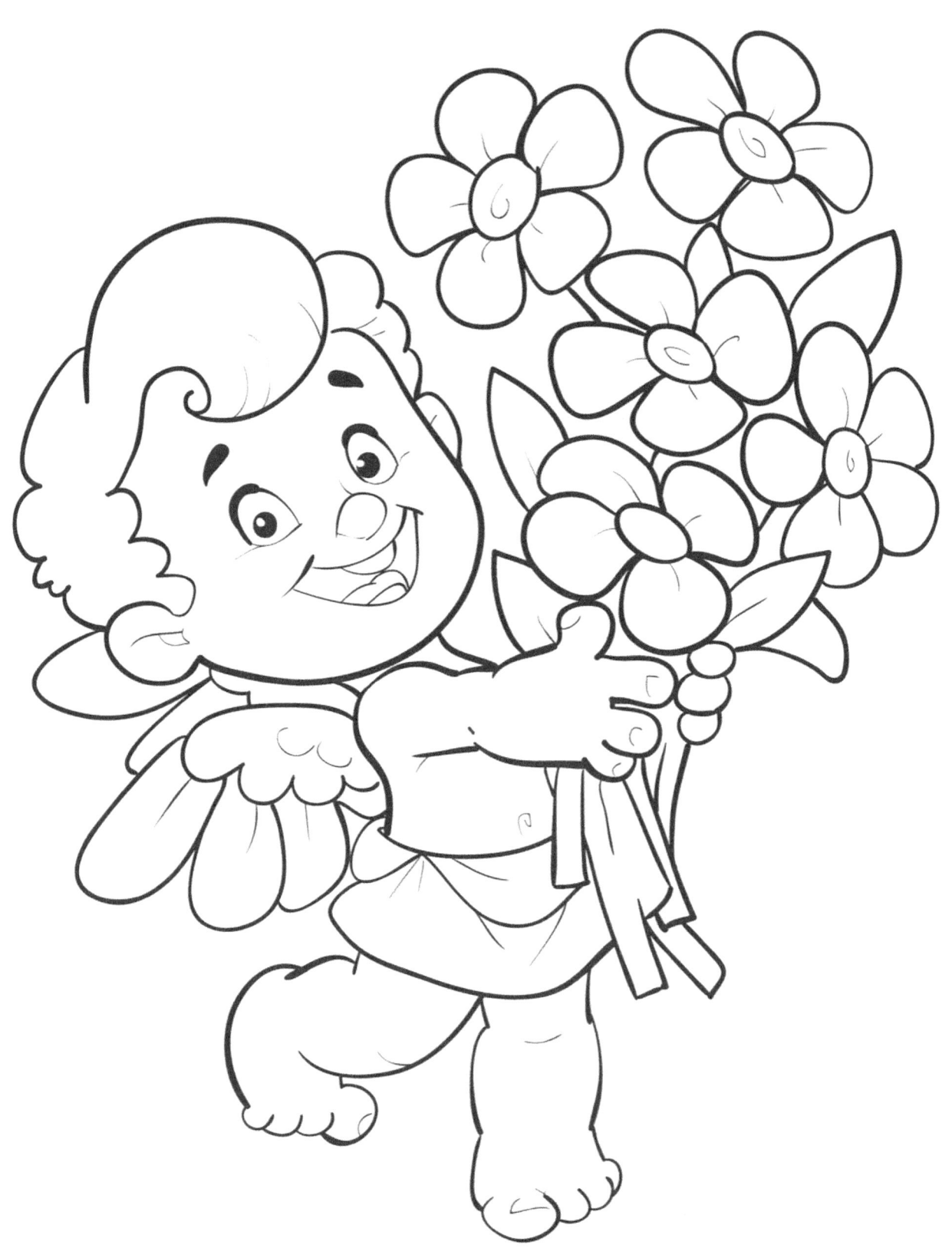

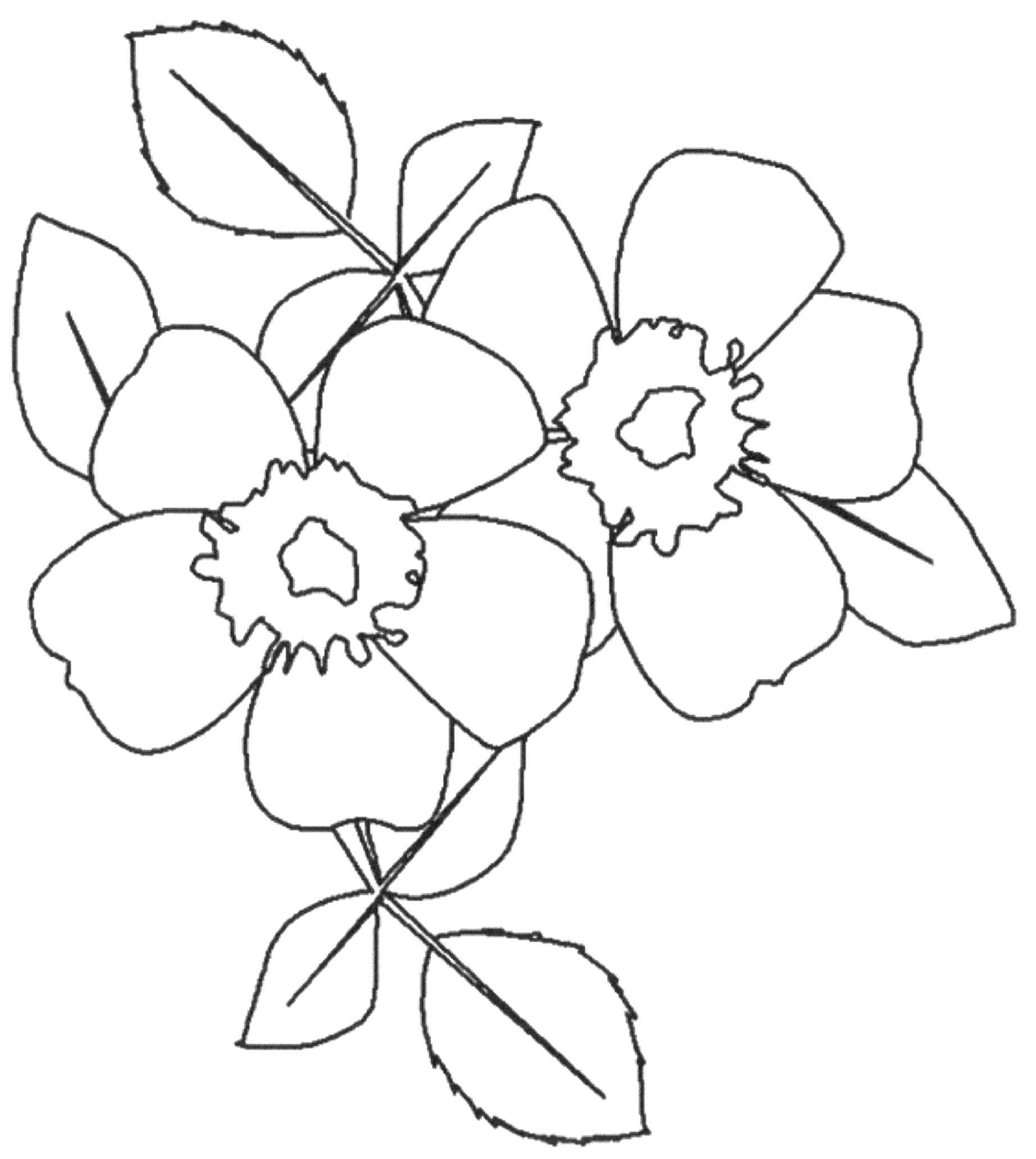

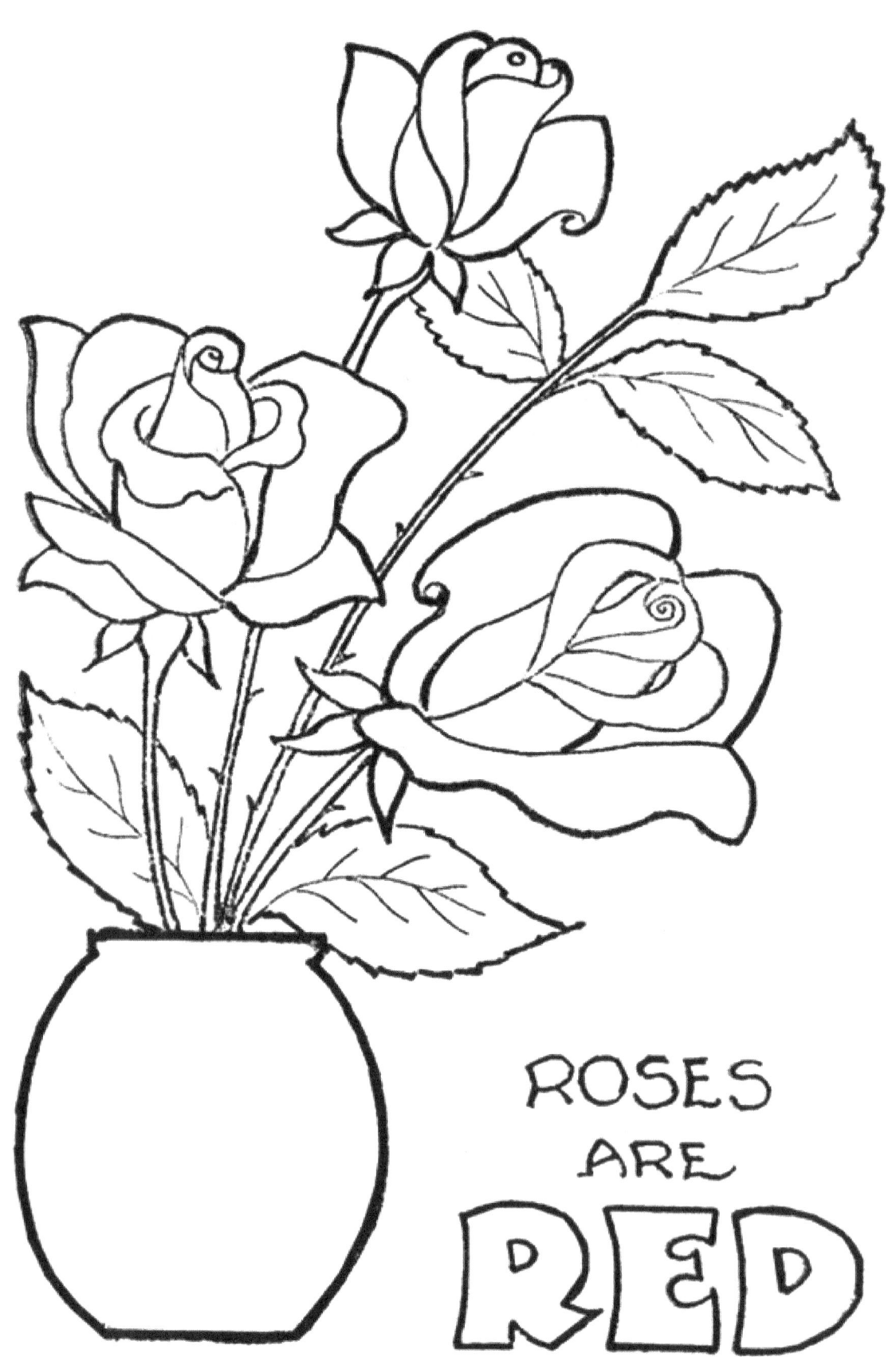

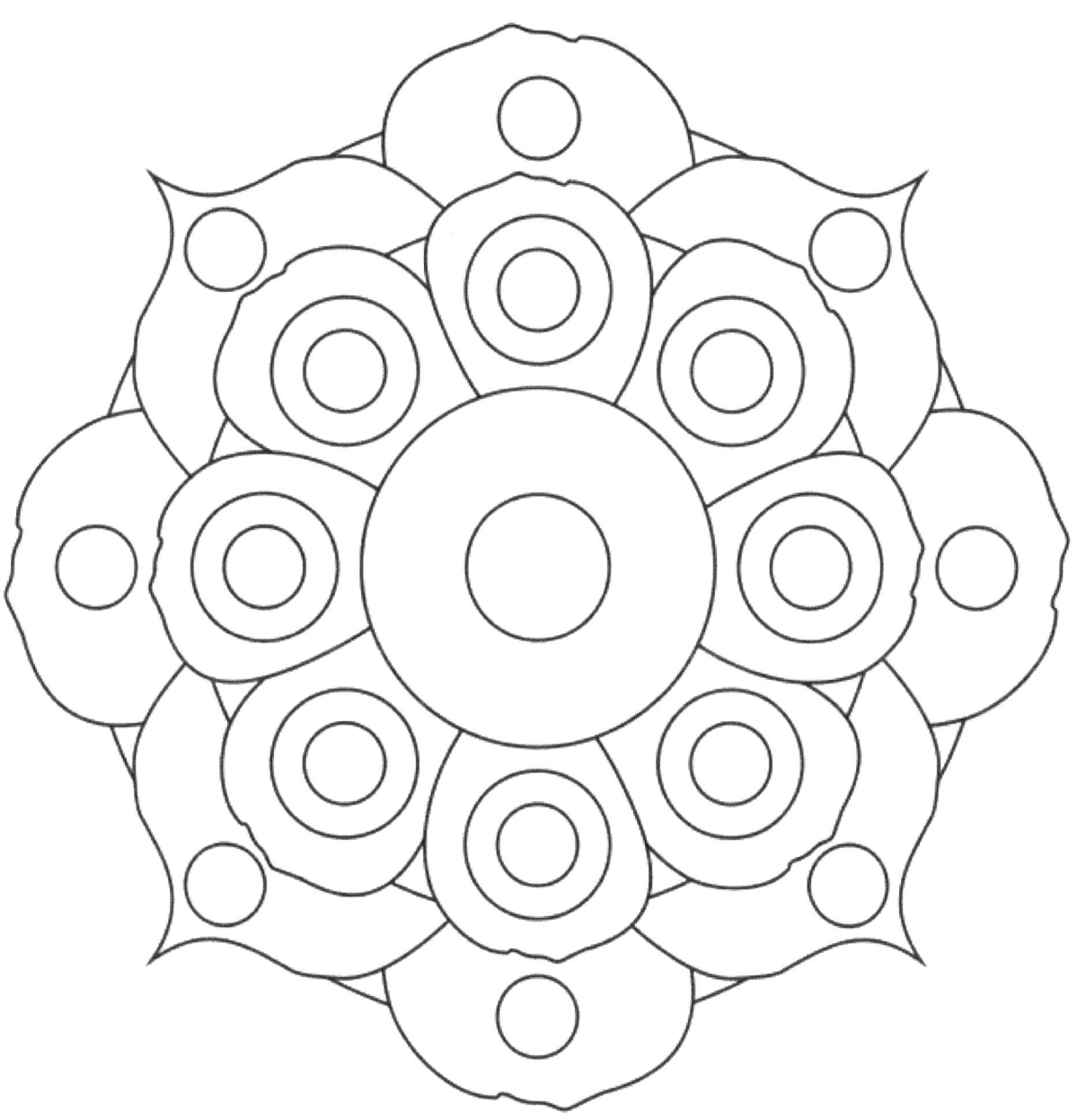

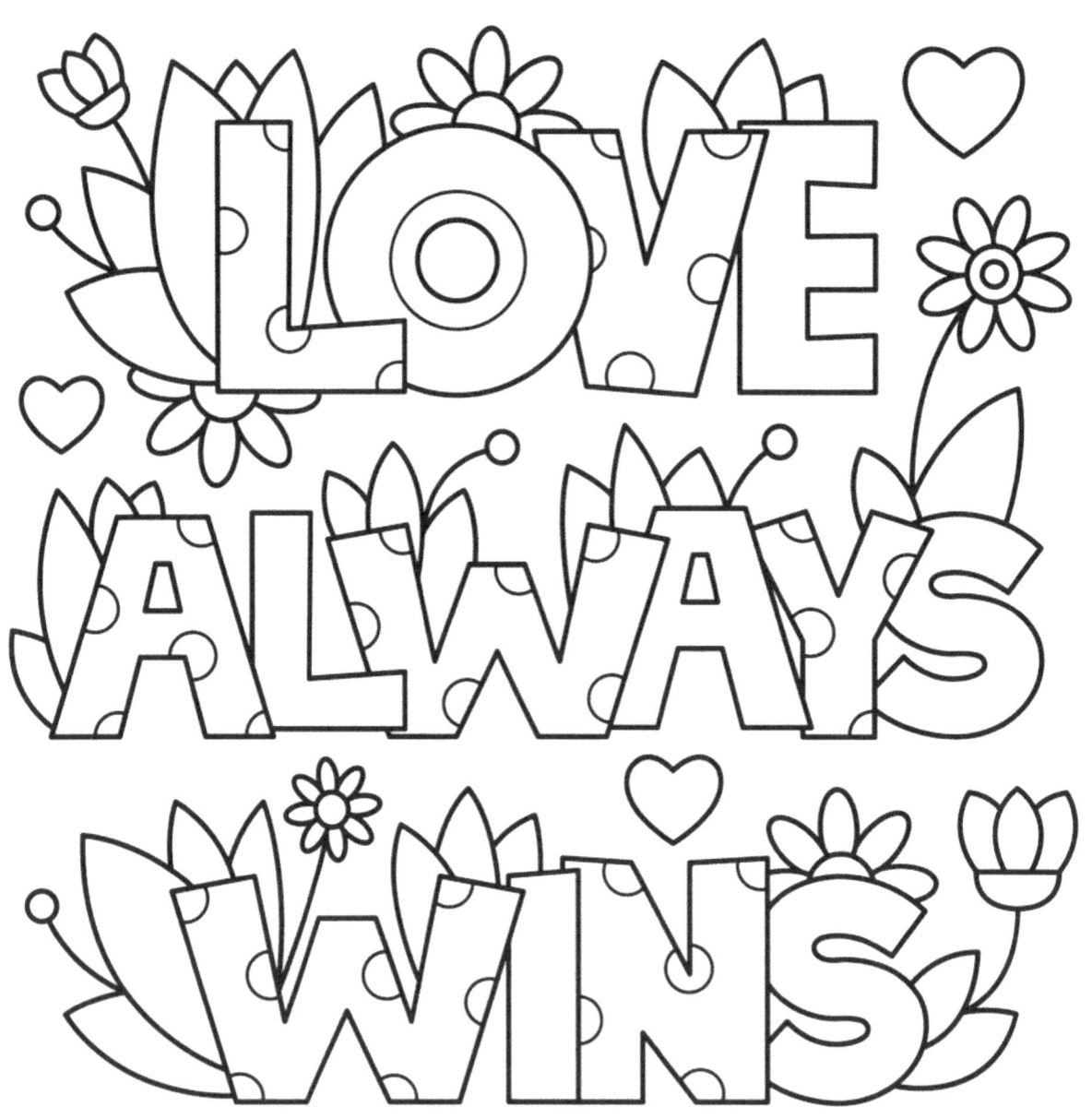